The Seafarers THE GREAT LINERS

Other Publications:

THE KODAK LIBRARY OF CREATIVE PHOTOGRAPHY
GREAT MEALS IN MINUTES
THE CIVIL WAR
PLANET EARTH
COLLECTOR'S LIBRARY OF THE CIVIL WAR
LIBRARY OF HEALTH
CLASSICS OF THE OLD WEST
THE EPIC OF FLIGHT
THE GOOD COOK
WORLD WAR II
HOME REPAIR AND IMPROVEMENT
THE OLD WEST
LIFE LIBRARY OF PHOTOGRAPHY (revised)
LIFE SCIENCE LIBRARY (revised)

*This volume is one of a series
that celebrates the history of
maritime adventure, from the Greek
trireme to the modern ocean liner.*

For information on and a full description of any
of the Time-Life Books series listed above, please write:
Reader Information
Time-Life Books
541 North Fairbanks Court
Chicago, Illinois 60611

The Cover: As a harbor pilot waves a
greeting, the Cunard Line's great *Queen
Mary* steams past the Ambrose
Lightship at the entrance to New York
Bay in this 1959 painting by Jack
Gray. With her sister ship, the *Queen
Elizabeth*, and the French Line's
magnificent *Normandie*, the *Queen Mary*
marked the culmination of a century
of ocean-liner development.

The Title Page: The ship's telegraph was
the vital link between the captain
on the bridge and the engine room many
decks below in the bowels of the liner.
This one, from the *Leviathan*, indicates
that the ship is under full steam.

THE GREAT LINERS

by Melvin Maddocks
AND THE EDITORS OF TIME-LIFE BOOKS

TIME-LIFE BOOKS, ALEXANDRIA, VIRGINIA

Time-Life Books Inc.
is a wholly owned subsidiary of

TIME INCORPORATED

FOUNDER: Henry R. Luce 1898-1967

Editor-in-Chief: Henry Anatole Grunwald
President: J. Richard Munro
Chairman of the Board: Ralph P. Davidson
Executive Vice President: Clifford J. Grum
Editorial Director: Ralph Graves
Group Vice President, Books: Joan D. Manley

TIME-LIFE BOOKS INC.

EDITOR: George Constable
Executive Editor: George Daniels
Director of Design: Louis Klein
Board of Editors: Dale M. Brown, Thomas A. Lewis,
Robert G. Mason, Ellen Phillips, Gerry Schremp,
Gerald Simons, Rosalind Stubenberg, Kit van Tulleken,
Henry Woodhead
Director of Administration: David L. Harrison
Director of Research: Carolyn L. Sackett

PRESIDENT: Reginald K. Brack Jr.
Senior Vice President: William Henry
Vice Presidents: George Artandi, Stephen L. Bair,
Robert A. Ellis, Juanita T. James, Christopher T. Linen,
James L. Mercer, Joanne A. Pello, Paul R. Stewart

The Seafarers

Editorial Staff for The Great Liners:
Picture Editor: John Conrad Weiser
Designer: Herbert H. Quarmby
Text Editors: Anne Horan, Sterling Seagrave
Staff Writers: William C. Banks, Gus Hedberg
Chief Researcher: Martha T. Goolrick
Researchers: Regina Cahill, Patti H. Cass,
Philip B. George, W. Mark Hamilton,
Katie Hooper McGregor, Elizabeth L. Parker,
Blaine McCormick Reilly
Copy Coordinators: Sheirazada Hann, Elise D. Ritter
Art Assistants: Santi José Acosta, Michelle Clay
Picture Coordinator: Marguerite Johnson
Editorial Assistant: Adrienne George
Special Contributors: Barbara Hicks, Barbara Levitt,
Philip C. F. Smith (research)

Editorial Operations
Design: Anne B. Landry (art coordinator); James J. Cox
(quality control)
Research: Phyllis K. Wise (assistant director),
Louise D. Forstall
Copy Room: Diane Ullius (director), Celia Beattie
Production: Gordon E. Buck, Peter Inchauteguiz

Correspondents: Elisabeth Kraemer (Bonn); Margot
Hapgood, Dorothy Bacon (London); Miriam Hsia, Susan
Jonas, Lucy T. Voulgaris (New York); Maria Vincenza
Aloisi, Josephine du Brusle (Paris); Ann Natanson
(Rome). Valuable assistance was also provided by: Penny
Newman (London); Carolyn T. Chubet (New York).

The Author:
Melvin Maddocks has maintained a New
Englander's interest in ships and the sea.
His father was a ship chandler on Boston's
Commercial Wharf during the days of tran-
sition from sail to steam, and Maddocks
himself served on board Navy LSTs during
World War II. Harvard-educated, he is a
columnist and critic for *The Christian Science Monitor,* as well as a frequent contrib-
utor to *Time* and other magazines.

The Consultants:
John Horace Parry, Gardiner Professor of
Oceanic History and Affairs at Harvard
University, received his Ph.D. from Cambridge University. He served on destroyers and aircraft carriers in World War II,
rising to the rank of commander in the
Royal Navy. He has written 10 books, including *Trade and Dominion* and *The Dis-
covery of the Sea.*

Frank O. Braynard, a lifelong specialist in
maritime affairs, is best known as founder
and general manager of the Op Sail '76 review of tall ships in New York Harbor during the 1976 Bicentennial Year. He has
published 13 books and innumerable arti-
cles on such subjects as the early steamship *Savannah* and New York Harbor tugs,
and is completing a five-volume history of
the great liner *Leviathan.*

William Avery Baker, a naval architect and
engineer, spent 30 years with the Shipbuilding Division of Bethlehem Steel Corporation, designing vessels of all sizes up
to supertankers. He was later curator of the
Hart Nautical Museum at the Massachu-
setts Institute of Technology, where he
took his degree. He was also author of *The
Engine-Powered Vessel,* a history of ships
from the first paddle-wheeler to the first
commercial nuclear ship, the *Savannah.*

Library of Congress Cataloguing in Publication Data
Maddocks, Melvin.
  The great liners.
  (The Seafarers; v.4)
  Bibliography: p.
  Includes index.
  1. Ocean liners — History.   2. Ocean travel — History.
I. Time-Life Books.   II. Title.   III. Series.
VM381.M32   387.2'43'09   78-1366
ISBN 0-8094-2664-1
ISBN 0-8094-2663-3 lib. bdg.
ISBN 0-8094-2662-5 retail ed.

Contents

To ply the Atlantic in a grand hotel

The names alone were enough to evoke an aura of epic size and majesty—the *Leviathan*, the *Titanic*, the *Queen Mary*, the *Ile de France*, the *Normandie*. There were dozens more. They were the great liners. And in the decades between the turn of the century and the thunder of the jet age, they ruled the North Atlantic shipping lanes, transporting passengers by the millions back and forth between Europe and the United States.

Never in history had mankind fashioned such awesome machines. They were the largest objects that ever moved, and the most complex—the ultimate expression of the Industrial Revolution. Virtually every maritime nation with any pretensions to grandeur had to see its flag flying on at least one great liner.

Immigration fueled the era. The liners' lower decks—steerage it was called—were jammed with people fleeing the Old World for the New. But the vessels' greatness in the eyes of an admiring public lay elsewhere. Three quarters of their vast space was reserved for the upper classes—the rich, the royal, the famous and all the would-bes swimming in the wake of these personages. For them, a passage on a great liner was a week-long gala in a palatial grand hotel. A passenger might now have "the privilege of seeing nothing at all that has to do with a ship, not even the sea," as one brochure put it. The British went so far as to assert that "Going Cunard is a state of grace."

In their rivalry, shipping-line publicists and the graphic artists of poster lithography outdid themselves in abandon. Every liner appeared bigger, longer, more splendidly luxurious than the next.

The Cunarder *Mauretania* was a study in Edwardian elegance. The French Line's *France* was known as the "Château of the Atlantic," an orgy of Louis XIV opulence with sweeping staircases, marble fountains, and stewards in Moorish pantaloons pouring Turkish coffee. The Hamburg-American Line's *Amerika* featured an upper-deck restaurant staffed by London's Ritz-Carlton and freshly stocked with the finest oysters, caviar and truffles (plus mushrooms and strawberries grown in an afterdeck greenhouse). The Italian Line's sunny *Conte di Savoia* had a Pompeian pool on deck surrounded by real sand, and marble interiors modeled on the Palazzo Colonna in Rome.

Life aboard was a dreamworld, detached from reality the instant the mooring lines were cast off. "Barring a bridle path for the equestrian, a smooth road for the automobilist and a forest for lovers to walk in, everything else seems to have been provided," said one appraiser of the *Mauretania*.

A first-class cabin on board the *Ile de France* might cost as much as $200, a princely sum during the Great Depression. And taste-maker Lucius Beebe wrote that "20 pieces of luggage were an absolute basic minimum for social survival." A traveler should count, Beebe wrote, on at least four changes of clothing per day.

But where else could one spend a week, as the Cunard ad put it, "that will leave you feeling like a duchess or a millionaire"? Where else could one rub elbows with both? Still, one was advised to choose one's liner with care. "The Queens who cross in the *Berengaria* are the more conspicuous Queens," a Cunard pamphlet maintained.

For some it was all just a bit much. Christopher Morley once remarked, "For seven days we had the universe to ourselves but even God, I think, was restless on the eighth." Yet most people gave themselves over to what Thomas Wolfe called "the supreme ecstasy of the modern world"—the voyage aboard the great liner, decks ablaze with light, promenades as wide as city streets, "all of this made to move upon the stormy seas, leaning against eternity and the grey welter of the Atlantic at 27 knots, all of this, with the four great funnels cut sharp and dark against the evening sky, burning with a fierce, exultant vitality."

Scarcely parting the waves, a flock of sea birds playing about her bow, the supreme Normandie crosses the Atlantic at the pinnacle of her success, as this poster proudly attests. Of all the great liners, the Normandie was generally regarded as the most beautiful—and according to the writer and inveterate traveler Ludwig Bemelmans, "more female than all other ships I have known."

8

The Aquitania, Cunard's flagship in the 1920s, glides into New York Harbor, a vision of majesty framed by skyscrapers.

Passengers waving, the Queen Mary, flagship of the merged Cunard and White Star lines, sets sail in the 1930s.

"Hamburg—Germany's greatest port—Hamburg-Amerika Line, Germany's greatest steamship line," brags this 1930s German poster.

Against a backdrop of Manhattan's Empire State Building, the North German Lloyd Line shows off three liners on the transatlantic run.

With Italian flair, a liner of the Cosulich group, eventually part of the Italian Line, courses past a symbolic American Indian in the 1930s.

Though not quite so large as some, the 28,300-ton flagship of the Holland-America Line offered immaculate quarters and impeccable service.

Challenging Europe for supremacy, the U.S. Lines in the 1920s promises all the superlatives associated with great liners.

The largest ship in the world

S·S· LEVIATHAN
United States Lines
managing operators for
UNITED STATES SHIPPING BOARD

Attended by a bevy of tugs, the pride of the U.S. Lines—a German war prize originally named the Vaterland—eases into her Hudson River berth.

First visions of a golden age at sea

etting forth from Quebec on her first trial runs along the St. Lawrence River in August 1831, the *Royal William* offered little to suggest that she was destined for greatness. Save for her illustrious name, that of the reigning British monarch, there was nothing the least bit regal about her. She was a strange vessel, a mongrel possessed of neither the grace of her ancestors nor the power of the vessels that would descend from her.

At first glance, she looked like a schooner, with a sharp bow bearing a long, lancelike bowsprit. Three tall masts rose from her deck. But amidships stood an aberration: a tiny smokestack poking its head timidly up between the towering masts. Beneath this stack were two huge paddle wheels, one on each side of the hull, churning the water to a froth. Once the stack and paddle wheels were visible, of course, the *Royal William's* true identity was clear: here was no sailing vessel, but a steamship, powered by coal-burning boilers driving pistons that in turn rotated those giant paddle wheels. With a steam pressure of five pounds per square inch, the *Royal William* could make about eight knots. Though she carried a full set of sails, they were for auxiliary use only. The wisp of smoke rising from her stubby stack proclaimed as clearly as a signature that here was a new breed of ship as different from the sailing ship as the railroad train, then making its debut, was different from the stagecoach.

The *Royal William* was not the first steamship, of course. French engineers had been experimenting with steam-driven craft as early as 1615, and a Glasgow instrument maker named James Watt had devised the first efficient marine steam engine in the early 1760s. A Frenchman, Claude de Jouffroy d'Abbans, constructed a steam-powered vessel that in 1783 managed to run for 15 minutes against the current of the River Saône. And in 1807, Robert Fulton had sent his historic *Steamboat* up the Hudson River 150 miles from New York to Albany in the startling time of 32 hours. With Fulton the age of steam had begun.

In 1811, the *New Orleans*, designed by Fulton, became the first steamboat to travel the Mississippi. Within a decade, steamers were making 1,200 visits a year to New Orleans. On the Hudson River, steamers of 1,000 tons commonly carried 600 passengers in a semblance of style on the Albany run. In Europe, passenger and cargo steamers traversed the English Channel, the Irish Sea and the Baltic, and were commencing service in the Mediterranean. In 1819 an American vessel, the *Savannah*, equipped with an auxiliary steam engine, became the first to experiment with steam on an Atlantic crossing, using her engine for a short distance *(page 20)*. But no one had attempted a crossing of the North

Surrounded by boatloads of well-wishers, the Great Western steams out of Bristol harbor in 1838, inaugurating the first regular transatlantic steamship service. After a fire had marred her shakedown cruise, only seven passengers braved the initial voyage. But her popularity grew; during the next eight years she carried thousands of travelers.

Atlantic relying almost entirely on the newfangled steam machines.

That was left to the *Royal William*. In August 1833 this small, ungainly, tentative vessel, only 176 feet long, displacing less than 500 tons, secured her place in the annals of the sea by becoming the first vessel to steam virtually all the way across the Atlantic, paddle-wheeling the 2,500 miles between Nova Scotia and London in a little less than a month. In so doing, she ushered in a whole new era of seafaring—not that anyone was much aware of it at the time.

In fact, the *Royal William*'s arrival in London was scarcely noted. No bands greeted her passage up the Thames. No dignitaries delivered grandiloquent speeches. No honors were accorded her builders or her captain on this historic voyage. Why should there have been? The *Royal William* had started life with no ambitions of becoming the first transatlantic steamship. And her passage across that great ocean was nothing more than happenstance, a simple act of desperation on the part of owners seeking to rid themselves of an unprofitable ship.

When she slid down the ways at Quebec in April 1831, the *Royal William* carried hopes only of being the flagship in a fleet of Canadian steamers flying the colors of the Quebec and Halifax Steam Navigation Company. As the firm's name implied, she was to connect Quebec to Halifax and other Nova Scotia ports. But she became a financial disaster. Cholera swept Canada in 1832, and the *Royal William* was quarantined for months when the disease broke out during a passenger run to Halifax. By the time the plague flag was lifted, her debts were so huge that she was sold at auction for £5,000, less than a third her cost. Her new owners, anxious for a quick profit, tried to sell her in Boston. They found no takers. Only then did they think to gamble on a transatlantic passage, hoping to unload this voodoo ship on the more active London market.

Thus on August 17, 1833, the *Royal William* chugged out of Pictou, Nova Scotia, and shaped a course east toward her destiny. In view of what was to transpire in the century ahead, her passage was ludicrous.

Paying $20 each (wine not included), a scant seven travelers made up the passenger list. The *Royal William* carried an equally small cargo, featuring a harp and a collection of stuffed birds in a box that a certain Dr. McCulloch was sending to London to be sold as "natural curiosities" of Canada. The dominating presence aboard the ship was 324 tons of good Nova Scotia coal. For nobody knew exactly—or even inexactly—how much fuel a two-cylinder side-lever engine would require to paddle-wheel across the Atlantic in this unprecedented way.

In command of the *Royal William* was Captain John McDougall, about whose early career little is known—except that he apparently spent much of it enjoyably ashore, pottering about his house and garden in Quebec City. Logically, everything about the first Atlantic steam crossing ought to have driven him back to the snugness of home and harbor. But Captain McDougall was obviously the kind of man who thrives on adversity. Off the coast of Newfoundland the *Royal William* was hit by a vicious storm. The captain in a letter later reported: "We experienced a gale of wind which rather alarmed my engineer; he wished very much to go into Newfoundland. We had previously lost the head of the foremast, and one of the engines had become useless from the beginning of the

The Royal William, first to conquer the North Atlantic by steam, churns steadily upwind without sails in 1834 while a sailing ship passes in the background. With 200-horsepower steam engines turning 18-foot paddle wheels at 20 revolutions per minute, the Royal William could cruise the ocean at a leisurely eight knots.

gale; with the other we could do nothing and the engineer reported the vessel to be sinking. Things looked rather awkward." Awkward was scarcely the word for it. What saved the *Royal William* was her sailing-vessel rigging; the long heavy spars helped to stabilize her as sea poured over her decks and sent her rolling precariously to and fro.

As the gale at last eased off, Captain McDougall, helped by his reluctant engineer, managed to pump the vessel free of water; then he headed his battered ship eastward again, with her one engine thumping. It was 10 days before McDougall could repair and fire up the other engine. "After that," he declared cheerfully, "we got on very well."

Pretty well, anyhow. About every four days, McDougall had to turn off the *Royal William's* engines and rely on sails for a while in order to clean salt deposits from the boilers. After almost three weeks at sea he had to put in at the Isle of Wight for further repairs: the boilers were leaking badly. He also took the time to spruce up his ship with a fresh coat of paint. Thus he could brag that when he chugged up the Thames 25 days after his departure he did so "in fine style." He had come 2,500 miles across the Atlantic, most of it by steam, at an average speed of four knots.

The *Royal William* never made another Atlantic passage. Shortly after her arrival in London, she was sold for £10,000, double what her own-

A bold experiment with the "Savannah"

When Moses Rogers, shown in silhouette, was fitting out his ship to cross the Atlantic, scoffers called it "the steam coffin."

"Ship on fire!" came the urgent message from Cape Clear off the southern coast of Ireland on June 17, 1819. Immediately, His Majesty's cutter *Kite* set out under sail from the nearby Cove of Cork. But strangely, the cutter could not overtake the smoking vessel. Finally, after the cutter fired several cannon shots, the American ship *Savannah* heaved to, and the mystery was solved: she was running under steam.

Though steamboats were fairly common in coastal waters, no one expected to see a vessel steaming in from the open Atlantic. As it turned out, the *Savannah* had not exactly crossed the Atlantic by steam—that honor awaited Canada's *Royal William* in 1833—but she had made history by being the first ship to supplement sail power with steam on a transatlantic voyage.

The *Savannah* was under construction as a sailing packet in 1818 when she was spotted in a New York shipyard by Moses Rogers, a coastal steamboat captain who dreamed of a steamship line across the Atlantic. Rogers bought the 98-foot vessel and set about installing paddle wheels and a one-cylinder engine.

The small, 90-horsepower steam en-gine was never supposed to be more than a stand-by; the paddle wheels were even collapsible, so they could be stowed safely away from heavy seas. Rogers provided accommodations for 32 passengers in 10 tiny staterooms.

A crowd of cheering Georgians wel-comed the *Savannah* when she ar-rived in her namesake port on April 6, 1819, but the passenger trade that had been hoped for never did materialize. The mere idea of sailing the Atlantic while fires blazed away belowdecks daunted many people. Facing finan-cial difficulties, Rogers decided to sell his ship—but in Europe, so that he could still take her across the Atlantic.

The *Savannah* sailed on May 24, 1819, carrying only coal and firewood for her engine. The engine was run an average of four hours a day for the 29 days it took to cross from Savannah to Liverpool. On a number of occasions, sail and steam were combined to push the ship to a speed of 10 knots.

Finding no buyers in England, Rog-ers traveled on to Stockholm, where Sweden's King Charles IV offered him $100,000 in trade goods for the Savan-nah. But Rogers declined and sailed to Russia, where he hoped for cash from the Czar. Again no cash offers were forthcoming. Finally, he took the ship home, arriving in Savannah at the end of November 1819.

By now, Rogers was deeply in debt, and after trying in vain to sell the *Sa-vannah* to the United States Navy, he unloaded her at auction for a pittance to a small New York packet line. Her new owner immediately removed her engine, and she coasted between the ports of New York and Savannah for a year—carrying passengers at a prof-it for the first time—before she ran aground on Long Island.

As for Captain Rogers, he returned to river steamers. While piloting a boat on the Pee Dee River in South Caroli-na, he fell ill with fever—and slowly succumbed, at exactly the time his be-loved *Savannah* was starting to break up in the pounding Long Island surf.

A hybrid design, the Savannah had standard rigging but sported two paddle wheels, and a smokestack that was twisted to keep sparks from the sails.

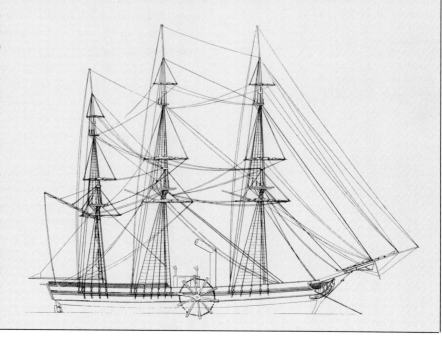

ers had paid, which pleased them mightily. She eventually wound up as a cruiser in the Spanish Navy, until her timbers were found to be rotting and she was left to decay in 1837.

Yet this little provincial steamer from Canada, so uninspired in her beginnings, so casually abandoned to her fate, represented an idea that would not sink. For 25 days as she thumped across the Atlantic, the *Royal William* had carried the future in her churning paddle wheels. Long after he returned to pottering about his house in Quebec, Captain McDougall remembered the taste of a heady new ambition—not just to cross the Atlantic and survive but to get there with speed and a certain "fine style." And so he presaged all the great-liner men to come, possessed by a common dream of converting the cruelest of open seas into a magic carpet on which a floating palace might swiftly glide.

"Floating palace," "greyhound," "leviathan"—the favorite metaphors for the ocean liner signaled the expectations behind her. She was an epic idea whose epic time had come. For a century after the *Royal William* first poked her bow tentatively out into the Atlantic, the masterminds of steamship travel built ever-bigger leviathans, ever-swifter greyhounds, ever-more-luxurious floating palaces. The wood of the *Royal William*'s hull gave way to iron, then steel; the paddle wheel was replaced by screw propellers; and the little roundhouse dining room, which looked like a pillbox, became a painstaking replica of the Ritz, with Escoffier's cuisine to match. By the turn of the century, "hotelism" was the catchword of the liners. Saloons resembled ballrooms at Versailles; every liner of any pretension boasted a swimming pool—modeled, naturally, on the baths of Caracalla, or Pompeii. Indeed, to be at sea was not to be at sea at all—as the French Line, with magnificent arrogance, indicated by calling its flagship *Ile de France* the "Boulevard of the Atlantic."

There were times when this boulevard was a rocky road indeed. For all its growing size and technological sophistication, the liner, after all, was a ship and the North Atlantic could act like a wrathful god. "Among the gifts to humanity," wrote the maritime historian E. Keble Chatterton, "there is not included that of taming the sea." The grim truth of the liner's vulnerability was demonstrated repeatedly, never more terribly than on the night of April 14, 1912, when the *Titanic*, a liner supreme, carried 1,503 people to their deaths after brushing an iceberg.

Yet such catastrophes, if not forgotten, had no visible effect on the burgeoning Age of the Great Liner. At their flood tide in the 1930s scores of huge luxury liners flying the colors of more than 20 commercial fleets and a dozen nations were regularly crossing the Atlantic in less than five days. For however long she reigned, the fastest vessel would hold the "Blue Riband"—a silver chalice emblematic of her supremacy in speed (*page 158*). In comparison with the *Royal William*'s bare handful of passengers, the great liners would routinely carry over 2,000 paying customers on each trip, and they were housed, fed and cosseted en route by as many as 1,200 crew members. In size 160 times the tonnage of the early steamers, one of these spectacular floating palaces, the French Line's *Normandie*, could swallow two *Royal Williams* end to end in her grand dining room alone. Such size and luxury were not at the expense of profit. In the late 1940s, in a fantastic year for tourism, two great steamers flying the flag of Britain's Cunard Line would earn their company the staggering sum of $50 million.

That was only proper, for the man who had founded the line, Samuel Cunard, was one of the great pioneers of transatlantic travel by steamship. Together with another brilliant and determined entrepreneur—an American named Edward Knight Collins—he quickly understood the promise of the *Royal William*'s voyage and moved swiftly to make that potential a reality. To Cunard goes the accolade for providing the first regular, dependable service across the Atlantic; even in his lifetime, it became an institution. And while Cunard was building his colossus, Collins rose boldly to challenge him by offering not only regular passage, but service fit for a king—or a millionaire. It remained for a third visionary—Charles Parsons, an engineer and inventor of genius—to provide the incredible power necessary to propel the great liners across the ocean at the speed of a bird. Among them, these three men were the pillars on which the Golden Age of the Great Liners rested.

It is a curiosity of history that Samuel Cunard's name appears among the first stockholders in the *Royal William*. A young Halifax businessman when he invested in her, he undoubtedly lost money on the vessel. But he followed her fortunes, and when she made her historic transatlantic crossing he obviously saw profits to be made in duplicating the feat on a regular basis. For Sam Cunard was nothing if not alert to commercial possibilities, and he had always been a man of the sea.

Cunard was born in 1787 in an unpainted shack a stone's throw from Halifax Harbor, and his first sights, sounds and smells were of the sea. His view of the world, as soon as he could sit up and look out the window, consisted of square-rigged merchantmen laden with molasses from the West Indies, fishing schooners out of the Grand Banks, whalers from New England and English privateers, not infrequently with a captured French ship in tow. Farther out, frigates and cruisers of the Royal Navy rode at anchor. A ferry carried passengers across the mile-wide harbor to Dartmouth, and presumably the first music the child heard was the eerie tooting of ferrymen blowing on West Indian conch shells to urge their customers on board.

As a youngster, Sam picked dandelion greens to sell after school. He hawked coffee and spices door to door. He ran errands and carried letters. At school he disliked elocution and saw no use for Greek or Latin. But he was a marvel at anything to do with figures. Cunard was scarcely 21 when he bought his first ship, the schooner *White Oak*, a British privateer's prize that he used in coastal and transatlantic trade. By the time the War of 1812 broke out, Cunard owned a 40-vessel fleet that profitably carried mail and cargo between Halifax, Newfoundland and Bermuda. Cunard's Wharf became a center of Halifax commerce.

Cunard married a rich man's daughter (Susan Duffus' father made a fortune tailoring military and naval uniforms during the War) and built a four-story house overlooking Cunard's Wharf. The little settler's cottage where he was born was converted into servants' quarters.

After the War, Sam expanded and diversified. He invested in timber,

Halifax businessman Samuel Cunard, his imagination fired by the emergence of steamship navigation, played a leading role in the founding of the first transatlantic steamship line in 1839 and saw it grow into a colossus. The soul of confidence, he liked to say: "We have no tunnels to drive, no cuttings to make, no roadbeds to prepare. We need only build our ships and start them to work."

coal, brickyards, fisheries—anything that promised a fair return. In 1838, at the age of 50, Sam Cunard was a multimillionaire and the father of seven daughters and two sons whom he shepherded into the front pew of St. George's Church each Sunday. Was it not time to relax, to retire to a country house with calfbound books and crystal chandeliers and peacocks on the terraced lawn? Evidently not.

Behind the perfect disguise of the cost accountant, there was a touch of the gambler in Cunard. In the early days, not once but three times, he had backed whaling expeditions to the South Seas. None of them turned a profit. As far back as 1831, the year the *Royal William* was launched, Cunard had reflected on the potential of steamships and had decided that transatlantic "steamers properly built and manned might start and arrive at their destination with the punctuality of railroad trains on land." The *Royal William* had subsequently proved that the Atlantic could be crossed by steam, and by now a number of vessels had been specifically designed for transatlantic service. One of them in fact, the *Great Western,* operated by a British railway company of the same name, was doing precisely what Cunard had proposed: carrying out a regular schedule of voyages between Bristol and New York. For Cunard, the gamble and challenge were irresistible: he would beat these frontrunners at their game; he had, after all, suggested the game years before.

In January 1839 Cunard left Halifax and the comfortable circle of past achievements and traveled to London to convince the British Admiralty that a self-made Nova Scotian was just the man they were looking for when they advertised for a contractor to carry mail on a monthly schedule across the Atlantic by steamship.

The actress Fanny Kemble, meeting him at a London dinner party, found Cunard "shy, silent, rather rustic." But there was something Napoleonic in his diminutive stature and self-confident air. He had a way, one observer noted, of making "both men and things bend to his will."

Operating out of a borrowed office in Piccadilly, Cunard wrote the Lords of the Admiralty: "I hereby offer to furnish Steam Boats of not less than 300 Horse Power to convey the Mails from a Point in England to Halifax and back, twice in each month." Furthermore, he would have his ships ready by May 1, 1840, performing as agreed for £55,000 per year.

Cunard wrote another letter to the best marine engineer of the day, Glasgow designer Robert Napier. To snobs of the London press, Napier, the son of a blacksmith, was, despite his achievements, "a mere provincial engineer"—a dabbler in "country-made engines." But Cunard knew that the painstaking Napier had built durable engines for paddle steamers, plodding on schedule, year in, year out, to the Isle of Man. Napier was a superb craftsman. "Every solid and known improvement that I am acquainted with shall be adopted by me"—that was his promise.

Napier had an ambition equal to Cunard's. Even before the *Royal William* made her crossing, Napier was persuaded that the future of the Atlantic belonged to the steamer. In 1833, he had written to a London banker proposing a transatlantic steamship company operating Napier-built vessels. "I would have everything connected with the machinery very strong and of the best materials, it being of the utmost importance to give confidence at first, for should the slightest accident happen so as to prevent the vessel making her passage by steam, it would be magnified by the opposition. But if, on the other hand, the steam vessels are successful in making a few quick trips at first and beating the sailing vessels very decidedly, then you may consider the battle won."

Cunard could not have put his own philosophy better. From the start he sensed that Napier was his kind of man. When he went north to meet him, he knew he was right. Cunard and Napier made a deal: the engineer would build three 950-ton vessels, with engines capable of 375 horsepower, for £32,000 each. "I have given him the vessels cheap," Napier confessed to a friend.

He had given them too cheap, and he had second thoughts. Napier was not greedy for money. He was greedy for excellence, and he decided that these first vessels to cross the Atlantic on schedule must be bigger, stronger than first conceived. Cunard had instructed Napier: "I prefer plain woodwork in the cabin, and it will save a large amount in the cost." Napier got the message, but he also understood that Cunard appreciated the value—the ultimate economy—of solid, substantial goods. He was as right about Cunard as Cunard had been about him. But the new specifications—raising tonnage to 1,139 and horsepower to more than 700—required greater capital. Cunard had also decided on a fourth ship. In sum, the cost might now come to well over £200,000.

At this point Napier introduced into the plot a couple of his fellow Scotsmen, George Burns and David McIver, as potential investors in Cunard's ships. Burns and McIver were already partners in the City of Glasgow Steam Packet Company, which operated Napier-powered steamboats between Glasgow, Liverpool and Belfast. On the Belfast run, for the benefit of their more anxious customers, Burns and McIver regularly included a priest as part of the crew. Such canny attention to detail was characteristic of them.

Napier, Burns and McIver sat down to dinner with Cunard: four provincials, thirsting to expand their parameters but playing things close to the chest. Certainly nobody was going to commit himself to anything without sleeping on it. "As talking after dinner generally ends in nothing," Burns wrote later, "so it did on this particular occasion." McIver in particular was worried that profits would be swallowed up by fines the Admiralty was prepared to levy if mail was late. But the whole idea had seized the cautious four by the scruff of their imaginations.

The next morning the quartet had breakfast at Napier's house. The rituals of prudence had been observed, and it was now propitious for the representatives of old Scotland and new Scotland to agree. Cunard put up £55,000 of his own, and a week later Burns, McIver and 32 of their friends came up with the rest, totaling £270,000 to capitalize the entire company. There were some minor political problems: English shipowners belatedly awoke to what was happening and petitioned the Admiralty for first consideration on the ground that Englishmen had a moral right to carry English mail. But the Admiralty turned them down. By early May, 1839, Cunard had a seven-year contract in his pocket and Napier had his order for the first transatlantic Cunard liners.

Not satisfied with his heady conquest of British civil servants and Scottish businessmen, Cunard set out to win over the United States.

The powerful steam engines and towering paddle wheels of the Cunarder Persia are shown in every detail in this elegant cutaway illustration, done by a naval architect in 1860. With her 40-foot paddle wheels assisted by sails on occasion, the Persia crossed from New York to Liverpool in a record nine days, one hour and 45 minutes, averaging 14 knots.

Under the original Admiralty contract, Boston was to be merely a feeder station for Halifax. Communicating the hurt pride of Bostonians to the Admiralty, Cunard shrewdly obtained for himself an increase of subsidy (to £60,000 annually) that allowed him to guarantee direct service from London to Boston. In gratitude, Boston merchants promised him a pier with free facilities for 20 years.

On July 4, 1840, the *Britannia*, flagship of Cunard's first fleet, sailed on her maiden voyage from Liverpool to Halifax. Among the passengers— fewer than half her capacity of 124—were Cunard and his daughter Ann.

Cunard had issued written instructions to Captain Samuel Woodruff: "It is of first importance to the Partners of the *Britannia* that she attains a Character for Speed and Safety." The two sometimes opposing requirements would ring through the history of great liners. And with a true Scotsman's eye to frugality, Cunard urged the engineer to keep furnace doors shut as much as possible and to use the dampers judiciously. Also, with a view to proper maintenance and record keeping, to blow off the boiler "at regular intervals" and "count the revolutions of the Engines every two hours, putting them down in the Log."

The *Britannia* made that first crossing in 13 days and finished with a burst of speed, logging 273 miles during her last 24 hours. She docked at Halifax at 2 a.m., July 17, and seven hours later got under way again for Boston, where a "Cunard Festival" awaited her. Bands played. Cannon roared. The mayors of every sizeable city in New England, followed by foreign consuls and local politicians, led a welcoming parade. Two thousand paraders ended up attending a banquet that lasted—with speeches—for five hours. Josiah Quincy Jr., President of Harvard University, and Daniel Webster were featured orators, along, of course, with the British consul. Quincy told Cunard that "he had a head to contrive, a tongue to advocate, and a hand to execute." Not since the *Mayflower*, everybody agreed, had there been such a crossing. A song composed for the occasion built to the chorus:

Oh dear, think of a scheme, odd though it may seem—
'Tis sure to succeed if you work it by steam.

During the next year, the *Britannia* and her three sister ships made 40 crossings without failure. But the Cunard line could not lay much claim to luxury. Charles Dickens, who sailed on the *Britannia* two years after her maiden voyage, left an unforgettable impression of the vessel. His cabin, Dickens complained, was so tiny that his luggage would fit in it about as easily as "a giraffe could be persuaded into a flower pot." The dining saloon resembled "a gigantic hearse with windows." As for food, "very yellow boiled leg of mutton" and "a rather moldy dessert of apples, grapes, and oranges" were the *pièces de résistance*.

But each crossing, however uncomfortable, consolidated the steamship's claim to the future. There were still 150 sailing ships for every steamship plying the Atlantic. But the time of glory of the tall ships was coming to a close. One day in 1853, Donald McKay, the Michelangelo of the clipper ship, was exclaiming over his pride and joy, the *Sovereign of the Seas*, to a group of English shippers with whom he had just concluded business in his Boston shipyard. Expansively he invited them to sail back to Liverpool with him as his guests. The Englishmen declined. They were, they explained, taking the next Cunarder—to save time.

McKay was nettled. On the day Cunard's *Canada* sailed from Boston, the *Sovereign* left New York. McKay had put all his money and all his heart into the *Sovereign*. She was a glorious ship, capable of coaxing up to 20 knots from her 12,000 yards of canvas.

For five days the clipper led the way in stiff winds. On the sixth day the wind fell and the *Canada* consolidated all the gains that the Cunarders had been making. The puffing little steamship moved ahead of the *Sovereign* and slogged on for seven days more to reach Liverpool first by a margin of almost 48 hours. On that day Sam Cunard and his "tea-kettles," as one sea captain had scathingly referred to them, ruled the waves, and the Age of the Great Liner arrived, not as a series of episodes but as a way of life.

Still, Sam Cunard had one more rival to defeat before he could quit. He had won his bet on engines. But he was challenged now by a romantic out to make the liner look like the winner she was—by marrying to those dependable engines a measure of the glamor of a McKay clipper.

Measuring 30 inches high, with handles of cavorting dolphins, this ornate silver cup was Boston's gift to Samuel Cunard in 1840 soon after his flagship, the Britannia, completed the first of Cunard's regularly scheduled transatlantic crossings. Embossed with a view of the Britannia, the cup cost some $5,000, a considerable sum in those days, and was purchased with the donations of more than 2,500 proud Bostonians.

To the cheers of Bostonians, the Britannia steams out of her berth in the city's ice-locked harbor and glides along a specially cut, seven-mile channel to the open sea. The extraordinary lane—gouged by cutting devices known as ice plows—was devised by Boston businessmen determined to prove that their city, chosen over New York as Cunard's first American terminus, was a dependable port no matter the weather.

In September 1850, Jenny Lind, known as "The Swedish Nightingale," sailed for America on the steamer *Atlantic*, flagship of the new New York and Liverpool United States Mail Steamship Company. Waiting in New York for The Nightingale with dollars dancing like high notes in his head was Phineas T. Barnum, the great circus entrepreneur who had introduced Tom Thumb to the world in 1842. Barnum had arranged for a proper showman's welcome. "On the dock," he wrote, "a bower of green trees, decorated with flags," had been prepared for the tiny soprano, "together with two triumphal arches, one of which was inscribed 'Welcome, Jenny Lind!' The second was surmounted by the American eagle and bore the inscription 'Welcome to America!' "

To make certain that the open arms of America would appear to Jenny Lind as those of one man—Barnum—the endlessly scheming P.T. used his friendship with the health officer of the Port of New York to sneak aboard the *Atlantic* as she lay at anchor in quarantine off Staten Island. But when he was escorted to Miss Lind's stateroom, Barnum found himself a poor second. The Swedish Nightingale was almost hidden behind a bank of roses just presented to her by another American, Edward Knight Collins, the owner of the *Atlantic*.

Born in 1802 in the Cape Cod town of Truro, Collins had gone to sea in his teens and, so it was whispered, had brushed once or twice with

Caribbean pirates in the West Indies. In the 1830s he founded a successful sailing packet line he named, with dramatic flair, the Dramatic Line. His flagship was the *Shakespeare*, at 927 tons the largest merchant ship of its day to carry the American flag. The *Sheridan*—named after the author of *School for Scandal*—followed the same tonnage. Other Dramatic Line ships were named after players: the *Garrick*, the *Siddons*. Each ship featured a painted wooden bust of its namesake as figurehead. The theatrical was Collins' style.

Collins saw the steamship as both a sound investment and a splendid wager, and with his showman-like charm he talked the United States government into staking him. In 1847 he signed a government contract to carry mail between New York and Liverpool on a schedule of 20 round trips a year. For an annual subsidy of $385,000, Collins agreed to build five incomparable ships. The government thought it well worth the expense. Collins' assignment, in the words of Delaware Senator James Asheton Bayard Jr., was "to proceed with the absolute conquest of this man Cunard." Ohio Congressman Edson Baldwin Olds put it even more bluntly: "We have the fastest horses, the prettiest women, and the best shooting-guns in the world, and we must also have the fastest steamers." And, it seemed, the most opulent.

If early Cunarders had the awful austerity of English Channel ferries, Collins' liners seemed to inherit the flair of the Mississippi riverboat. The heart of Collins' fleet was the Atlantic Quartette, including the *Atlantic, Pacific, Arctic* and *Baltic*—each with a gross tonnage of 2,850, churning along at a speed of 12.5 knots, about 500 tons heavier and two knots faster than the rival Cunarders.

No luxury was spared. At a time when few homes boasted such amenities, Collins' liners were steam-heated and had indoor plumbing "with an apparatus for pumping up salt water from the Atlantic," as one awed traveler reported. This passenger noted too that there was a barbershop "with glass cases containing perfumery, etc., and in the center a 'barber's chair,' adjustable, with an inclined back and comfortable, well-stuffed seat." The vessels' interior woodwork was rosewood, holly and satinwood. The drawing rooms were heavily carpeted and furnished with plush armchairs and sofas and tables topped with Italian Brocatelli marble. Ceilings were carved and gilded. Windows were decorated with stained-glass designs emblematic of American freedom, and in the grand saloon of Collins' first steamship, the *Atlantic,* an oil painting surrounded by stars and spread eagles depicted the "female figure of Liberty gracefully trampling on a feudal prince," as one chronicler put it. Mirrors hung everywhere—a professor was disturbed when he looked up from his reading and faced six visions of himself. Even the spittoons on this early liner were prettied up to resemble sea shells.

There was an ice room containing 40 tons of ice on every Collins liner, and the variety and abundance of food matched the selections on a menu at New York's famous Delmonico Restaurant: green-turtle soup, turkey in oyster sauce, boiled bass in hollandaise sauce, goose in champagne sauce. There were fresh—not moldy—fruits and vegetables. For dessert the ship offered almond cup custard, apple fritters with hard sauce, red-currant tartlets. In short, if Cunard made the great liner practi-

Determination marks this portrait of American shipping magnate Edward K. Collins, whose steamers were dubbed "palaces of the ocean." Chosen by the U.S. government to compete against Britain's Samuel Cunard, Collins won a hefty subsidy to lure transatlantic passengers. "The United States has never yet done anything," claimed a Harper's editorial, "which has contributed so much to its honor in Europe, as the construction of this Collins Line of steamers."

At the fitting-out dock of a New York ironworks, workmen equip a newly launched steamer hull with the boiler that will power her engine and yet-to-be-installed paddle wheels. In 1848, when this lithograph was made, New York was one of the most important steamer centers in the nation; scores of steam-powered vessels plied the Hudson River and nearby coastal shipping lanes.

cal, Collins made her a luxury product. Passengers, for the first time on an ocean, could travel in style.

The problem was that style cost. In the first 11 months of 1852, Collins' liners carried 4,306 passengers as against 2,969 sailing on Cunarders. But it was an empty success; despite his mail contract and subsidy, Collins was operating at a huge loss. The government more than doubled his subsidy, to $858,000 per year. Yet for the full year 1852, the net loss came to nearly $1.7 million, a staggering sum in those days.

Speed was as great an obsession with the Americans as luxury—and as expensive. "Speed!" urged Delaware's Senator Bayard. "Speed against which these British can never hope to compete. Speed of such magnitude as the Government of Britain and its chosen instrument, this man Cunard, never visualized or could ever hope to achieve." By pushing the engines to the limit, Collins' captains could get a maximum of 13 knots from their vessels. On April 19, 1852, the *Pacific* became the first ship ever to cross the Atlantic in less than 10 days, making her westbound passage in nine days, 20 hours and 15 minutes. But the passion for speed burned up coal, burned out engines, and punished wooden hulls. Frantic repairs had to be made between crossings.

And now fate decreed a catastrophic blow. On September 20, 1854, the *Arctic* sailed from Liverpool with 233 passengers—among them Collins' wife and two young children. Around noon on September 27 the *Arctic* was proceeding at full speed, as usual, through a heavy fog off the

Grand Banks, making desultory honks on an inadequate foghorn. Suddenly the bow lookout gave a cry, and the *Arctic* crashed into the little 250-ton French steamer *Vesta*, en route to France. The *Vesta* was badly damaged, but her iron hull had done far more severe damage to the wooden hull of the *Arctic*. Disappearing into the fog, the *Vesta* headed for the safety of St. John's, Newfoundland, leaving the *Arctic* with three holes punched below her water line. With sails futilely draped over the gaping splits, the *Arctic* set out for Cape Race, 65 miles away. But water pouring into her engine room soon stopped her paddle wheels. She sank within hours. Only 86 of the 233 passengers and 175 crew members made it to shore in lifeboats or were picked up by passing vessels. In all, 322 were lost, including Collins' wife and the two children.

Less than 18 months later, on January 23, 1856, disaster struck again. The *Pacific* sailed from Liverpool with 45 passengers and 141 crewmen and was never heard from again—presumably the victim of ice floes that other ships described as descending on the North Atlantic that year like a drifting continent. Making a crossing two weeks later, a passenger on the *Atlantic* described a near miss: "At 7 o'clock in the morning, we saw a spectacle which none on board will ever forget; it was, in fact, the finger of Providence, and some more deserving than I and others must have been on board. The whole veil of fog rose like a curtain, and we looked upon an ocean scene beautiful, fearful, and grand. The atmosphere as far as the eye could reach was clear; the sun shone brightly on a continuous chain of icebergs about 100 feet high, intermingled with fields of ice. Chain after chain burst upon the sight, and the sight was awfully impressive. In less time than it has taken to write this, the curtain descended, and all became obscurity again." Wisely the captain steered south to skirt the icebergs, then headed west again.

Within a year and a half, Collins had lost two ships, and nearly lost a third. Confronted by heedless speed, the Atlantic Ocean had levied an awful toll. But Collins would not, perhaps could not profit from this lesson. He now proceeded to build his masterpiece, the *Adriatic*—bigger (3,650 tons), faster (15 knots), more opulent than anything before her. Two classes of accommodation were installed: 316 first class, 60 second class. She was launched in April 1856. But Collins continued to shoal waters financially; in Congress, voices were raised in outcry against his huge subsidies, and in February 1857 they were cut back to the original $385,000 per annum, which was hopelessly inadequate. Thanks to public horror at the disasters at sea, the euphoria of steamship travel was gone. Writing in *Harper's,* a journalist went so far as to suggest the unspeakable: "We had best stick to sailing ships and leave the steam navigation of the ocean to John Bull."

On November 23, 1857, as the *Adriatic* set forth on her maiden voyage, three tugs pulled her out of her berth carelessly, allowing her to be blown against the dock. Only the pier was damaged; however, it was not an auspicious beginning. Her design speed of 15.9 knots was attained in her first crossing. But Collins himself was moving even faster toward bankruptcy. Alarmed, the government withdrew support, leaving Collins to fend for himself. The *Adriatic* was to make only two voyages as a Collins liner before the creditors foreclosed.

The spartan appointments and minuscule space of this Britannia stateroom moved Charles Dickens, an 1842 occupant, to call it "an utterly impracticable, thoroughly hopeless and profoundly preposterous box." His bed, he wrote, was like a shelf: "Nothing smaller for sleeping in was ever made except coffins."

On April Fools' Day, 1858, the *Adriatic*, the *Atlantic* and the *Baltic*—all that remained of the Collins Line—were auctioned off for a mere $50,000 to James Brown, a major stockholder, who had lost two sons, a daughter and two grandchildren when the *Arctic* went down. The *Atlantic* and *Baltic* were chartered for service as army transports during the Civil War. After the War the *Atlantic* was scrapped. The *Baltic*, engines removed, was converted into a full-rigged sailing ship, carrying cargo for German brokers in the grain trade. The *Adriatic* became a mail carrier under the British flag, setting records between Galway and New York, before ending up as a storeship off the coast of Africa, where she was finally beached and left to rot. As for Collins, he lingered on, attempting one venture after another and failing in everything, until he died in 1878, impoverished and broken in spirit.

Just a year after Collins' collapse, Sam Cunard, 72 and still turning a tidy profit on the Atlantic run, became Sir Samuel Cunard, Baronet. At last he had nothing to prove. The Atlantic was "Cunard's Pond," and he could retire to an estate in Canada.

But the spectacular loser, Collins, had almost as great an effect on the

Passengers gathered in the grand saloon of the Collins Line's Atlantic in 1850 await refreshments carried by a steward who is entering through the arched doorway at rear. Travelers found the opulent drawing room—fitted with costly mirrors, rich carpets, inlaid woodwork and velvet-upholstered furnishings—not only elegant but also remarkably comfortable, for the Atlantic was the first liner with compartments warmed throughout by steam heat.

future as the solid winner, Cunard. Collins' dangerous, exhilarating dream—that a ship could be a kind of express-speed luxury hotel—became a permanent part of the heritage of the great liner. Cunard captains, mouthing their founder's policy, would still speak dutifully of placing safety before speed. But their engines were now tuned to cruise at more than 12 knots, and Cunarders like the *Persia*—built under pressure of Collins' competition—abjured the old cramped spartan simplicity in favor of "noble proportions" and what was promoted as "true Oriental taste." After Collins the liner could never be a plodding ferryboat—a simple functioning service. Speeding between two worlds, the great liner became a third world in itself.

The ambiance of the great liner—the tassled cord pull for the steward, the drapes disguising a porthole, the parquet and carpeting concealing the brute fact of a deck—none of this mattered to Charlie Parsons, the last, but certainly not least, member of the great liner triad. To Parsons, a liner was the engine room. A tale is told of how one evening in the midst of an Atlantic crossing, Parsons disappeared from the first-class lounge and was seen hurrying to the lower decks. Scrambling through bulkhead after bulkhead in his evening clothes, he hungrily made his way to the shaft tunnel and squeezed as near as he could to the propellers. Indifferent to the chill, the dampness, the oil, he crouched, listening to the music of the ship. When the chief engineer found him, Parsons engaged the officer in a discourse on torsional oscillations and harmonic vibrations, as if the two men were analyzing a Beethoven symphony.

If the liner as palace at sea meant nothing to Parsons, perhaps it was because from childhood he had known the real thing. Born in 1854, the year the *Arctic* met her doom, Parsons was raised in Birr Castle, Parsonstown, Ireland, the stately home that had been in his family since 1621. In these idyllic environs—surrounded by a moat and a park that included two rivers and an artificial lake—Parsons' father, Lord Rosse, an accomplished astronomer, constructed his own telescope at leisure. The example of the father was not lost on the son.

Parsons was a 19th Century phenomenon: the gentleman-scientist. At the proper time, he effortlessly took a distinguished degree in mathematics at Cambridge. But all of his life he would remain an amateur by temperament: a lover of machines for their own sake, who treated the world as his playground.

When he was a child, his mother recalled, Charlie Parsons would not eat unless he had a mechanical toy or at least a building block to play

Listing heavily to starboard, her stern awash and her bow timbers showing the damage caused by collision with the iron-hulled Vesta, the Collins Line flagship Arctic slowly sinks into a glassy sea off Newfoundland in 1854. This rendering of the disaster by Nathaniel Currier was made from a sketch by one of the few passengers who survived. The hero of the tragedy was Stuart Holland (inset), a young apprentice engineer who, on orders from his captain, stood alone on the bow, firing the ship's signal gun once every minute until the Arctic went down.

with. When he became a father himself, he was every child's delight. He designed a magical steam-powered tricycle he called "The Spider" for his daughter. Miniature locomotives of his invention propelled themselves along the library carpet, dripping alcohol and occasionally setting off a blaze. All inventions were toys and games to Parsons, and after experimenting with torpedoes and rockets, he finally dedicated himself to a toy of toys: the turbine engine.

The turbine was hardly a novelty in Parsons' day. It was, in fact, an older design than the reciprocating engines that powered the Cunard and Collins liners. In 150 B.C., the Greek inventor Hero had shown that steam could be harnessed to drive a series of blades mounted on a rotor shaft—in the same way that moving air can drive a windmill.

The practical problem was the velocity of a jet of steam. It was so high that it demanded blade and rotator speeds beyond the limits engineers could accommodate in a machine of any great size. This challenge caught Parsons' fancy. By mounting his blades on a series of wheels of increasing size, Parsons thought he had discovered how to control steam velocity in such a predictable way that a turbine could be built on a large scale and run at reasonable speeds without undue stress.

In 1884 Parsons built a turbine that drove a generator, producing 7.5 kilowatts at 18,000 revolutions per minute. This was the first successful application of turbine power to the production of electricity; in fact, a couple of years later, the chief constable at nearby Gateshead acquired a refined model of this Parsons turbogenerator and employed it to provide night lighting for the local ice-skating pond. Parsons might have pursued this breakthrough and become a utility magnate. However, he was much more interested in the sea. In 1894, when he was 40 years old, Parsons founded the Marine Steam Turbine Company and devoted the remainder of his long life to perfecting the steam turbine as a practical engine for a ship.

The refinement of marine propulsion systems in the preceding 50 years had been considerable. Engine-room boilers had evolved from square to cylindrical in shape, which brought a dramatic increase in the pressure they could withstand. The old paddle wheel was replaced by smaller, more efficient underwater propellers. In 1840 the paddle-wheeled *Britannia* had achieved 10.4 knots and 740 horsepower by bringing steam to a pressure of nine pounds per square inch; 41 years later, screw-driven *Servia* achieved 16.7 knots and 9,900 horsepower by bringing steam to 90 pounds per inch in a heavy cylindrical boiler. Furthermore, the screw propeller reduced the consumption of coal to 3.28 pounds per indicated horsepower, as compared with five pounds for the paddle wheel. But the steam engine itself, despite its refinement, remained fundamentally the same reciprocating cylinder-and-pushrod power plant that drove the *Royal William*.

A lover of lists, Parsons itemized systematically the vast advantages he expected a marine turbine engine to demonstrate over the conventional reciprocating engine: 1. Increased speed. 2. Increased carrying power. 3. Increased economy in steam consumption. 4. Reduced initial cost. 5. Reduced weight of machinery. 6. Reduced vibration. 7. Reduced upkeep, in terms of both money and manpower.

Bizarre ideas to sustain castaways

For all their ambitious speed and refinements, the early steamers were no less at the mercy of the sea—perhaps even more so—than the sailing ships they were replacing. In the first two decades after Samuel Cunard began regular transatlantic passenger service in 1840, no fewer than 13 vessels sank, with the loss of more than 2,200 lives. In 1863 one English traveler warily observed: "A trip to the States was held to be quite a serious enterprise. You made your will before you sailed."

It was only natural that interest should focus on lifesaving devices and that the ideas should be as ingenious as the technology that made possible an Atlantic crossing by steam. Alas, most of the contraptions were too impractical for general use. As before, passengers could only place their faith in flotation vests and wooden lifeboats that might or might not function in an emergency at sea.

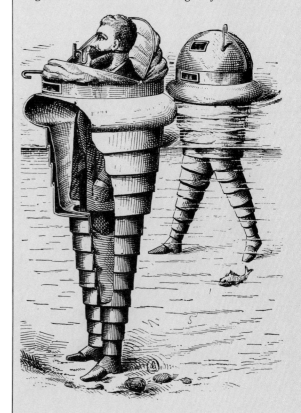

Heavy, waterproof sailcloth stretched over a jointed cylindrical frame was supposed to assure total shelter and indefinite flotation in this 1877 preserver devised by Traugott Beek of New Jersey. The hood stored a month's food and water supply and had an air pipe leading to the occupant's mouth. Metal-banded boots protected against injury from rocks and fish.

A tight-fitting rubber helmet with glass eye windows, this 1878 invention by Francis Cummerford of Delaware offered protection against the elements to both castaways and passengers on deck. A rubber mouth covering could be taken off to use the small megaphone supplied for long-distance hailing.

This floating tube with a breathing device was the 1886 brain storm of Philadelphian Joseph Badia. The tube was inflated by a vial of liquefied gas, which was released by wetting a soluble paper strip.

Once a castaway had deciphered the directions—keyed to letters and numbers on the drawing—for this 1868 rubber suit by John Stoner of New York, he could float erect in a cork jacket (I), change direction with a hand propeller (M) and enjoy food, drink and reading material stored in the flag-topped magazine (labeled "Fig. 2").

Ballasted to prevent capsizing, this large globular capsule, designed in 1877 by one J. Manes, had room enough for 50 people. In addition to a hollow mast for fresh air and a porthole for hoisting flags, there was a door to an outside gallery, for use by lookouts in fair weather. Propulsion was to be achieved by means of a propeller attached to a crank that was operated from within the cabin.

However, no less a personage than the Admiral of the Fleet, Lord John Arbuthnot Fisher, summed up what most experts thought were Parsons' chances of making good his list: "The majority of the marine engineers of the world looked upon the turbine as a wonderful piece of ingenuity but as a practical impossibility."

To Parsons, of course, this only served as a delightful challenge. He had a laboratory set up in his country home at Holeyn Hall, Wylam-on-Tyne. Here, followed about by a white sulphur-crested cockatoo, he set about building a turbine-powered vessel of incredible speed. First came hull design: long, narrow, with a knifelike prow. He began with a two-foot model, towed by fishing rod and line. Next came slightly larger models, propelled by twisted rubber bands and then by tiny turbines powered by alcohol fuel burning in boilers made of old biscuit tins. "It is blowing hard today," he wrote his brother at this stage. "I tried the model in a quarry close by, with comparatively big waves—it cut right through them like a knife."

Gradually the toy evolved into a bigger toy: the 100-foot *Turbinia*, only nine feet wide and weighing a mere 44 tons. To drive this splinter of a vessel, Parsons experimented with seven different engines. He wound up linking three turbines to reuse the same steam in succession—the "triple expansion" system—developing an astonishing 2,100 horsepower. To transmit this power, Parsons tried various propeller designs

Last of the steamers fitted with auxiliary sail, Cunard's Etruria, launched in 1885, is framed in this engraving from a Cunard handbook by the distinctive funnel and flag of each major contemporary steamship line and the colorful pennants representing the international code of signals. At the turn of the century, funnels on a vessel became a matter of prestige and a few liners boasted four huge stacks—one or two of which were dummies.

in all sorts of combinations, finally ending up with triple-bladed propellers mounted on three shafts.

With infinite patience—changing a tolerance here, an alloy there—he worked up the *Turbinia*'s speed from 20 to 34 knots. During the *Turbinia*'s tests, Parsons himself manned the controls. In the tiny engine room there was only space for one man at a time to swing his shovel. Fanned by Parsons' exhortations, the fireman would shovel as fast as he could until he ran out of breath. Then he would retreat outside, gulping air, while the next man took his turn.

After three and a half years of trial and error, Parsons was, at last, ready to audition his *Turbinia*. One June day in 1897 he got his chance. The occasion was the Grand Naval Review, in celebration of Queen Victoria's Diamond Jubilee. The might of Her Majesty's fleet was drawn up in the waters off Spithead. The Prince of Wales, the future Edward VII, was on hand—dressed as Admiral of the Fleet—along with Prince Henry of Prussia, the Kaiser's brother.

Parsons sneaked the *Turbinia* in among the small craft herded off to one side as spectators. Then, as Prince Edward appeared aboard the royal yacht and bands struck up the national anthem, Charlie Parsons made his move. Calling for full speed, he shot out from the spectator ranks and raced down the review lane alongside the mammoth battleships. There was, an onlooker recalled, a big wave, a black bow and a flame of fire shooting from the stack—the whole thing traveling at nearly 35 knots. Nobody had ever seen man move over water that fast.

A picketboat futilely attempting to intercept the intruder lost her aft ensign when Parsons suddenly turned and whipped in behind her, passing so close astern that the *Turbinia*'s bows clipped off the Navy boat's ensign staff. Toward the end of the run there was another close shave. All through the action, the *Turbinia* had been towing her ship's launch behind her (there was no room on deck). And now, as the *Turbinia* nimbly maneuvered around, the launch broke loose and went smashing into the side of a sleek French spectator yacht. Recounted one of the *Turbinia* crewmen later: "I remember well the flow of language from the skipper, French and English."

Charlie Parsons had once written: "If you believe in a principle, never damage it with a poor impression. You must go the whole way." His "mad dash of Nelsonic impertinence," as the *Times* of London described it, offended the well-developed sense of etiquette of the Lords of the Admiralty. Fortunately their explosive language could not be heard by Queen Victoria, who was on the terrace of Osbourne House on the Isle of Wight, watching the fracas through a telescope. Before disciplinary action could be taken, Prince Henry of Prussia sent Parsons his congratulations and asked for a rerun. The *Turbinia* was an international triumph.

In the end, the Admiralty was impressed enough to commission Parsons to build two destroyers, the *Viper* and the *Cobra*. On her trials on Friday, the 13th of July, 1900, the *Viper* made a run of 37.11 knots. But a year later, in dense fog, she foundered on Renouquet Island near Alderney. She was going only 16 knots when she hit rocks. In 45 minutes her engine room flooded, and half an hour later all hands abandoned ship. The 210-foot hull then split as neatly as if it had been sliced.

On September 17, a little over a month later, the *Cobra* put out from Newcastle on another routine cruise. At 5 the next morning she hit bad weather, rolling heavily. She lowered speed to 10 knots. At 7 a.m., off Outer Dowsing Shoal near the Lincolnshire coast, the *Cobra's* crew felt a shock. The mate of the Outer Dowsing Light Vessel later testified that he saw the *Cobra* "coming from North, plunging heavily." At 7:15 a.m. he "saw steam blowing off from the third funnel aft, and immediately saw steam issuing from all parts of the vessel." At 7:20 a.m. he "saw her settling down in amidships as though she had burst; and 7:30 a.m. saw her sink stern first." There was "too much wind and sea," he said, "to render her any assistance." The survivors—only 12 of them—were not picked up until 6 p.m. Fifty-seven men were lost, many of them Parsons' friends. A diver went down 10 fathoms to inspect the wreck. She had suffered the same death as the *Viper*. At the court-martial the diver testified: "About 150 feet from the stem, the ship was broken entirely off like a clean cut right through." The flaw was entirely structural. In no way could Parsons' turbines be held responsible.

Shipbuilders are among the most superstitious of men. The *Viper* and *Cobra* disasters delayed the coming of the marine turbine engine. But they could not stop it. Four years after Spithead, a Scottish coastal steamer operator put a Parsons turbine into the *King Edward*, doing passenger service on the Clyde. That same year a small transatlantic operator, the Allan Line, commissioned the first turbine-driven oceangoing liners, the *Victorian* and the *Virginian*. In 1905 the great Cunard Line built the turbine-powered *Carmania* and followed with the two ships that confirmed once and for all Parsons' invention: the *Mauretania* and the *Lusitania*, launched 10 years after the *Turbinia's* impromptu exhibition.

The giant ship had found her giant engine. The seven promises Parsons had made for the marine turbine engine were kept, plus one he had not made, noted by an Admiral of the Fleet, Sir Charles Madden, after Parsons had been knighted at 72: "Sir Charles Parsons conferred the greatest benefit perhaps on the engine-room hands, whose duty it had been to slap the rapidly revolving crank-heads to be sure they ran cool. Those of you who can recall an engine room of this type will remember the stoker counting his fingers after each encounter with the whirling crank-head and hoping he would still have ten after the trial. Now, all is peace, whatever the speed, in the turbine engine room."

Sir Charles Algernon Parsons died at 77 on February 11, 1931, aboard a ship, the *Duchess of Richmond*. The scene was idyllic—Kingston Harbor, Jamaica, at sunset. As he slipped away quietly in his bunk, the only possible thing Parsons could have missed was the sound of an engine.

In the 75 years between the *Royal William* and the sister ships *Lusitania* and *Mauretania*, the liner had developed its attributes separately, one by one. Like figures in a morality play, Cunard portrayed Dependability (the virtue that made the 19th Century machine behave like a middle-aged puritan), Collins represented Elegance (the deliciously guilty self-indulgence of the Gilded Age) and Parsons stood for Power (the aphrodisiac of the years to come). With the *Lusitania* and the *Mauretania*, these separate attributes became a trinity and the apprenticeship of the great liner was over.

A curling wake marking her trail, the radical turbine-powered Turbinia dashes at 35 knots through ranks of British battleships during an uninvited performance at the 1897 Grand Naval Review. The Admiralty was furious, but the exploit by inventor Charles Parsons (below) gave the world its first look at the remarkable power produced by steam turbines, soon to become the principal source of propulsion for ocean liners.

The distinguished marine historian E. Keble Chatterton at the turn of the century tried to remind himself that, for all their awesomeness, the *Mauretania* and *Lusitania* "are *ships*, which have to obey the laws of Nature, of the Great Sea, just as the first sailing ship and the first Atlantic steamship had to show their submission." But these most recent Cunard liners compared to the first Cunard steamer, the *Britannia*, in terms of power (68,000 horsepower) on a scale of 34 to 1, in terms of tonnage (32,000) on a scale of 27 to 1, and in terms of passenger capacity (2,335) on a scale of 20 to 1. "There is nothing comparable to them," Chatterton was driven finally to conclude, "there are no standards whatsoever by which to judge them."

When the *Lusitania* began her maiden voyage from Liverpool the evening of September 7, 1907, more than 200,000 people crowded the waterfront to see her off. "Never before in the history of steam navigation had so much interest been excited," a journalist observed. Not only the seafarer but the man in the street seemed to sense that the art and science of the great liner had come to full bloom.

As if approaching the millenium, Chatterton summed up the *Mauretania* and *Lusitania* from the pinnacle of 1907: "And so we come to these two leviathans." Neither he nor anybody else would have believed at the time that in a brief half-dozen years another leviathan would come down the ways, 50 per cent longer, 50 per cent heavier, with almost twice the passenger capacity.

The "Great Eastern": a Titan among minnows

Wearing shoes and trousers spattered with dockyard mud, designer Isambard Kingdom Brunel pensively chews a cigar in front of the launching chains of the Great Eastern, the 18,915-ton luxury liner he fondly called his "great babe." As he roamed through the shipyard, overseeing building and fitting out, Brunel wrote copious memorandums, which he often stuffed for safekeeping into his top hat.

Victorian England loved nothing so much as extravagance, be it ashore or afloat. Gargantuan size, dazzling glitter, monumental expense and technological complexity on a hitherto undreamed-of scale—all these filled the Victorian breast with a triumphant sense of having mastered the world. Nowhere was this appetite more lavishly indulged than in the *Great Eastern*.

When she was launched in 1858, the *Great Eastern* was five times the size of any ship afloat. Her iron hull was 693 feet long, and everything about the £1,000,000 Titan was outsize. She boasted no fewer than five gilded and mirrored saloons, the grandest encompassing 3,000 square feet. With 800 cabins, some having their own bathtubs and hot and cold running water, her passengers were offered lodging fit for the Queen herself. The whole was to be propelled through the ocean at a mind-boggling 18 knots by twin 58-foot paddle wheels plus a 24-foot screw propeller mounted on the stern. Watching this creation take shape at Millwall on the Thames, one editorialist found her a "wise and obedient fulfillment of the designs of Providence."

The *Great Eastern* was the brain child of Isambard Kingdom Brunel *(left)*, a pioneering engineer who had already made a name for himself on both land and sea. In 1835 he built the Great Western Railway running from London to Bristol. And in 1838 he built the *Great Western* steamship, which was the first to offer regular service across the Atlantic. The *Great Eastern* was designed with an even more ambitious route in mind: Brunel originally planned to have her run between Britain and Australia as the *ne plus ultra* of ocean travel. He supervised every aspect of her construction, constantly improving and refining.

But the great ship never made a single voyage to Australia. Instead, she was put on the Atlantic run, where traffic was growing explosively. Despite the boom, the huge vessel could not pay her way. Her 4,000 berths were never filled; she was beset by costly accidents and bankrupted a number of companies. But for better or worse, the British public loved her. When after a series of metamorphoses she was reduced in the final days of her 30-year career to a tawdry fun fair, one observer, remembering her great expectations and the elegance of her youth, mourned: "Let her be decently buried beneath the wild billows of the great Atlantic. I for one will contribute to her funeral expenses."

Dwarfed by the Great Eastern's 58-foot-high hull, officials and crew gather for the first attempt at launching the ship on November 3, 1857. The launching, no less than the building, taxed Victorian ingenuity to the limits. Since the ship was almost as long as the Thames was wide at Millwall, she had to be launched sideways. It took two hydraulic presses three months to nudge her by inches along the 330-foot distance from her cradles to the river.

Novel webs of woven iron

For all her extravagant appointments, the *Great Eastern* had a most practical reason for being: the scarcity of coaling stations east of industrial Europe. "Nothing more novel is proposed," wrote Brunel when he put his idea to the Eastern Steam Navigation Company, than "to build a vessel of the size required to carry her own coals."

Though reliance on sail had not yet passed *(right)*, the plan for the ship was considerably more unusual than Brunel's modest appraisal suggested. First, the hull was constructed of two iron "skins" placed 2.8 feet apart; it was further divided transversely by 10 watertight bulkheads at 60-foot intervals, and longitudinally by two more that ran the length of the engine and the boiler rooms.

That design made possible a frame large enough and strong enough to carry 3,000 tons of coal. There remained the problem of generating sufficient power to move such a colossus. Brunel solved that by utilizing both the screw propeller and the paddle wheel. Their engines, of 1,600 horsepower and 1,000 horsepower, respectively, could be run separately or together, as could the 10 boilers and 100 furnaces that kept them going.

Two drawings—thought to be by the hand of John Scott Russell, who built the ship to Brunel's specifications—give sectional views of the Great Eastern on a scale of one inch to 42.33 feet. They show in miniature the ship's details, from the lumps of coal in the mighty bins belowdecks to the quilted velvet upholstery in her magnificent saloons above.

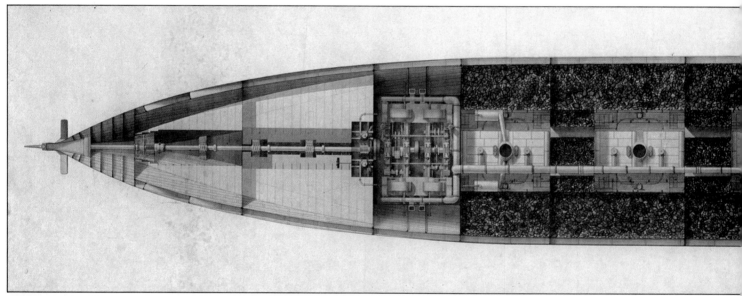

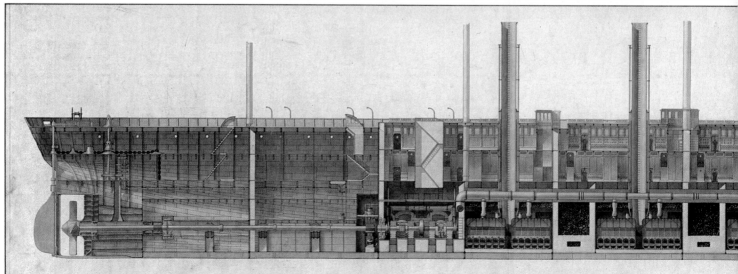

Under full sail, the Great Eastern
carried 6,500 square yards of canvas on six
masts. It took 80 men five hours to raise
or strike this great rig, but fortunately for
them, that did not often happen. The
sails were only for auxiliary power—when
the iron boilers had to be cleaned—
and were seldom used when the five stacks
were puffing smoke, contrary to this
fanciful 19th Century German lithograph.

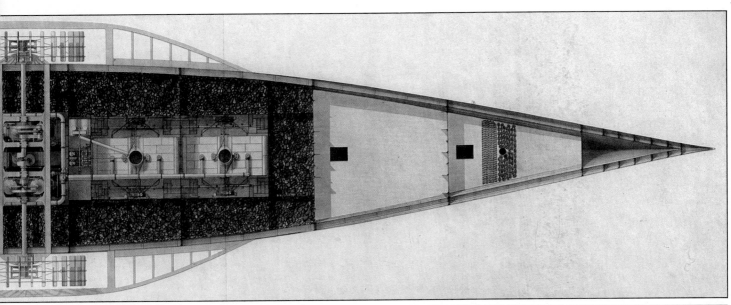

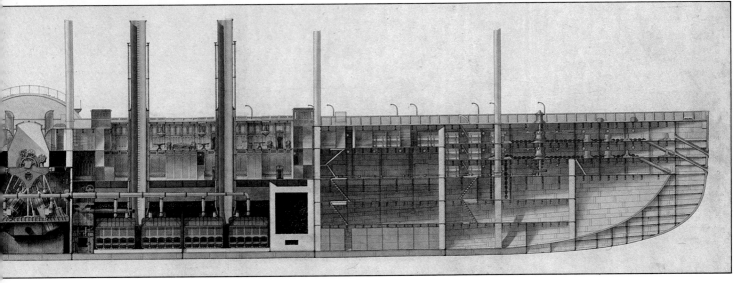

Prey to nature's caprice—and human foibles

None of the technological innovations that went into the *Great Eastern* could make her immune to the caprices of nature, nor to human error.

The first of several accidents occurred on her trial run down the English Channel on September 9, 1858. As the London *Times* correspondent reported the incident: "There was a confused roar amid which came the awful crash of timber and iron mingled together in a frightful uproar, and then all was hidden in a rush of steam." Someone had carelessly left the paddle engine's stopcocks closed, allowing the pressure to exceed the limits and causing a massive explosion; 15 crewmen were killed or injured.

But Brunel's ingenious design of multiple bulkheads saved the ship. The damage was confined to the boiler room, the scene of the explosion, and to the decks directly above.

Another disaster struck on a voyage in 1861, when the *Great Eastern* ran into a storm that ripped off her steering shaft and both paddle wheels, leaving her helpless in the churning sea. This time the passengers were the victims; among them they suffered 25 broken limbs. Many injuries were sustained in the Grand Saloon, where frightened people seeking companionship were battered by ricocheting furniture. Repairs to the ship took eight months and cost her owners £60,000.

Toppled by a boiler explosion, a smokestack lies in two pieces amid other debris on the Great Eastern's deck during her test run in the English Channel on September 9, 1858. Despite this calamity, the well-designed ship sailed on under power from other propulsion units.

The Grand Saloon lists to a horrifying 40° during an Atlantic storm in this contemporary engraving depicting an 1861 crossing. The ship tossed passengers and furniture about like jackstraws. "Let anyone who has seen the towering sides of the Great Eastern understand that the top platform of the paddle boxes actually dipped the water," recalled one passenger, "and they will perhaps have a slight notion of the extent of the slope of the saloon floor."

A sideshow for gawking landlubbers

Throughout her life the *Great Eastern* was the object of an unquenchable curiosity among landlubbers of every class and station. Queen Victoria, her husband, Prince Albert, and Leopold, King of the Belgians, were among the thousands who came to gawk at her before she steamed out of the Thames. When at last she completed her maiden voyage and arrived in New York in June 1860, she was accorded a 14-gun salute, and the chimes of Trinity Church rang out "Rule Britannia"; a huge crowd jammed the waterfront, and at the pier, welcomers seized the hawsers and helped pull her in.

The irony was that only 38 passengers were aboard to thrill to this welcome, and the £25 apiece they had paid for the passage was but a fraction of the cost of her voyage. A series of interminable delays had so annoyed prospective passengers, possibly nervous about this giantess anyway, that there were wholesale cancellations.

Desperate to raise money, the ship's owners put her on display in New York. And as in England, she drew viewers by the fascinated thousands. In four weeks 143,764 visitors toured her wonders. At 50 cents a head, they paid a total of $71,882—far more than her passengers had paid (though still not enough to make her solvent).

Exploiting American interest in the Great Eastern, New England railroads and a steamer line offer excursions at half fare to New York City, where the ship was berthed for four weeks in the Hudson River after her maiden voyage in June 1860.

A British cartoonist in 1858 satirically depicted the Great Eastern as a fun fair. The jest was prophetic; in 1885 a Liverpool merchant bought the ship for £26,200—scarcely ¹/₄₀ of the sums that had been poured into her—and turned her into a floating carnival, complete with music hall and souvenir stalls. One sad admirer mourned her as "an arrow that has missed its mark."

Days of glory at last

The *Great Eastern* found her greatest success not as the floating palace that designer Brunel had envisioned but as a work horse. She did so thanks to another visionary—Cyrus Field, an American manufacturer who in 1857 undertook the astounding venture of connecting Britain and North America by telegraphic cable. After unsuccessful attempts with a pair of smaller vessels, he bought the bankrupt *Great Eastern* in 1864 and fitted her out for the monumental task.

Odd though it might have seemed, she was just the ship for the job. No other vessel was capacious enough to hold the 2,000 miles of cable necessary to span the Atlantic. And huge as she was, the *Great Eastern*'s unique combination of paddle wheel and propeller allowed her to pivot this way and that, and to inch forward or aft at the command of the helmsman—a god-send when, as happened four times, various pieces of apparatus failed and the cable disappeared more than two miles into the deep. At last, on July 26, 1866, she triumphantly brought the cable ashore at Newfoundland, and instant communication was possible between Europe and North America. Over an eight-year span, she laid five more cables, four under the Atlantic and one linking Aden and Bombay.

As the great ship's day of glory drew to a close, one pessimist said that her chief value had been "in demonstrating that there was a limit in steamships in the direction of size." He was wrong, of course. In another 40 years the *Great Eastern*'s size would be exceeded and her posh accommodations rivaled. If she never made her owners a farthing, the reason was largely that the *Great Eastern* was a luxury liner whose time had not yet come.

Stripped of velvet portieres, walnut furniture and mirrored walls, the Grand Saloon serves as a tank to hold 2,000 miles of coiled cable. Because the directors of the operation feared acts of sabotage (unnecessarily, as it happened), they took the precaution of requiring the crew to wear overalls without pockets so they could not hide cable-damaging devices.

The Great Eastern steams into Heart's Content harbor, Newfoundland, having laid the first transatlantic cable from Ireland. When the crew drew the end of the cable ashore, the men were so excited, recalled Daniel Gooch, chairman of the Great Ship Company, that they "held it up and danced around it, cheering at the top of their voices."

The fateful odyssey of Hull No. 212

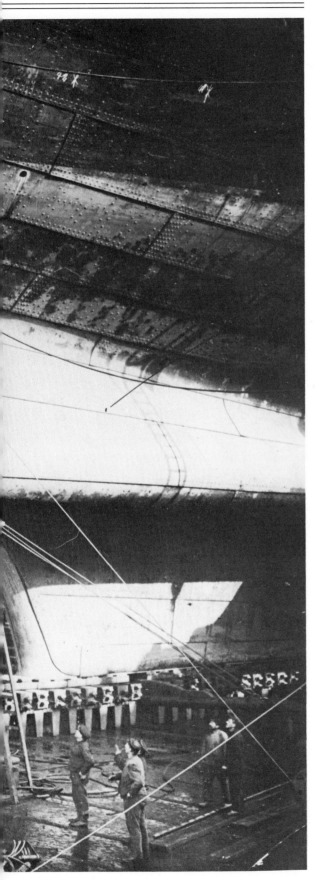

arly one September morning in 1911 a workman at the Blohm & Voss shipyard of Hamburg drove the first rivet joining the first two keel plates of what had been designated Hull No. 212. The joining of the first keel plates is to a ship what the laying of a cornerstone is to a building: a dedication and a beginning, a ritual and an act of honest toil. Pride, hope and concern were present at that particular moment, all the emotions that accompany any birth.

And what a colossal birth. The keel plates were Gargantuan—33 feet long, 78 inches wide and 1.36 inches thick, of noncorrodible chrome-nickel steel. The rivets that joined them weighed five pounds apiece and were so huge that they could be set only by Herculean hydraulic devices measuring twice the size of a man and suspended by cranes. Three million rivets of comparable size would eventually be pounded home, for here was no ordinary ship. Hull No. 212 was destined to be the world's largest vessel, indeed the largest moving object ever created by man, as its owners, the Hamburg-American Line, proudly pointed out.

The raw materials that went into the making of this 950-foot ocean liner still stagger the mind: 34,500 tons of rolled steel, 2,000 tons of cast steel, 2,000 tons of cast iron, 6,500 tons of wood. When she was finished, her gross tonnage would be a monumental 54,282 tons, a good 9,000 tons more than that of her nearest competitor, Britain's soon-to-be-launched *Aquitania*. And it would be 11 years before a greater great liner would be completed.

The Teutonic ambition behind Hull No. 212 was matched by Teutonic planning. Before that first rivet was sunk, five books of specifications were printed—the longest being 242 pages. Every fitting, every item of equipment was listed. The specifications for the ship's bells may be taken as a model of the thought that went into the ship. There were to be five bells "cast in the best bell metal, turned and polished" with the "ship and home port name engraved thereon." The bells—three of 24 inches in diameter, one of 14 inches, one of 32 inches—"shall be suspended quite freely so that the sound is not held back on any side." That 32-inch bell, weighing 529 pounds, was a fog bell to outpeal all fog bells.

In addition to the five books of specifications, an awesomely complete set of drawings had been prepared, some of them sketched on linen. One deck plan was a virtual mural, 10 feet long. The soul of an artist hid behind the straightedge of the draftsman. Each porthole was shaded with dozens of vertically drawn lines, as if an open-sea sun were shining idyllically on the glass.

Hull No. 212 slowly grew to meet her specifications. Two years after she was begun, an electric crane with a capacity of 250 tons lowered the boilers into her engine room. To drive her, the biggest and most modern steam plant of its kind was assembled. The 46 coal-fired boilers operated at 235 pounds of pressure per square inch, which translates into a mighty 61,000 horsepower. As transmitted to the water by four gigantic propellers, each 19 feet, seven inches in diameter turning at a stately 180 revolutions per minute, this awesome power would thrust the Hamburg-American Line's pride through the ocean at a speed of 23 knots, faster than any liner before her.

A launching verifies what the first joining of plates promises. It marks the first climax in a ship's history—the moment when a landbound carcass slides into its element at last and becomes, in fact, a ship. On April 3, 1913, flags decorated the buildings of Hamburg. Ferries carried crowds to grandstands along the Elbe River. Every rooftop with a view was crawling with spectators. Prince Rupprecht, son of the Bavarian Prince Regent Ludwig, was on the scene, dressed in spiked helmet and a buttoned-up army coat that bulged with his sheathed sword. The Mayor of Hamburg recalled the slogan that had summoned to arms the people of Prussia against Napoleon: "With God—for King and Fatherland."

On cue, Prince Rupprecht came forward and smashed a champagne bottle against Hull No. 212, crying: "I christen you *Vaterland*"—as if no less inclusive name would do for this minicontinent.

Propped between two cradles 40 feet high, the immense liner slid down the ways. The friction produced a halo of steam as her keel hit the water, making her look to the spectators watching from small craft in the harbor like a sea monster suddenly conjured up for the occasion by the whim of the gods.

One man's imagination had conceived the *Vaterland*. He was a man with a mind of enormous stretch, capable of the most vaulting visions even while applying full attention to the smallest detail. At the launching, Albert Ballin, managing director of the Hamburg-American Line, had stood behind Prince Rupprecht—his short, almost mousy presence, nearly overwhelmed, in fact, by his huge top hat. Yet Ballin was a man to be reckoned with, a fanatic obsessed by one idea: to produce the perfect ocean liner. He had been preparing for this glorious day all his life, tirelessly refining his dream, detail by detail. When he was not hard at work in his office overlooking Hamburg harbor, Ballin was equally hard at work at sea aboard one of his many Hamburg-American liners, relentlessly jotting down in a notebook the shortcomings he invariably found:

"Toast to be served in a napkin—hot."

"Notices on board to be restricted as much as possible, those that are necessary to be tastefully framed—sailing lists and general regulations to be in passengers' lists."

"State cabin on *Kaiser Friedrich*: no room for portmanteaux, trunks."

"*Deutschland*: dirty-linen closet too small; butter dishes too small."

Even when he was relaxing, Ballin paid attention to details. Playing a game of bridge in the smoking room, he would interrupt himself to jot a reminder: Why not have the Hamburg-American Line crest imprinted

In immaculate attire, with boiled collar and pearl stickpin, Hamburg shipping magnate Albert Ballin exudes the confidence of a lifetime of success in this portrait. By gaining for Germany a star role in world shipping, Ballin won the admiration —and friendship—of Kaiser Wilhelm II, who glowingly described him as a "clairvoyant and indefatigable pioneer."

Soaring eight stories above the launching ramp at the Blohm & Voss shipyard, the 36,000-ton hull of the Vaterland slips gracefully backward into Hamburg harbor, steadied by a wooden cradle on either side of the bow. Despite a checkrein of heavy cables and chains, she generated so much friction that she entered the water with a great hiss of steam, visible along the keel.

on the backs of the cards? Retiring to his cabin at last, the perfectionist would record one more thought before going to sleep: The pillows should be softer, plumper.

By the time the vessel made port, the notes, transcribed into a memo labeled "Obligatory," would be in the hands of the chief steward, the chef and all the others Ballin wished to have polish their ways.

The youngest of seven children of Danish-Jewish parents, Ballin had been born in 1857 barely 100 feet from the Hamburg waterfront. Five years before, his father had founded a small, not very profitable agency engaged in booking passage to the New World for emigrants flocking to Hamburg, not only from Germany but from Poland and Russia as well. None of the boy's several older brothers exhibited much interest in their father's business, nor did Albert at first. Music was his hobby; he played the cello.

When Albert was 17, his father died. An older brother took over the agency for a short while, but it showed every indication of foundering and he abandoned it to Albert. The Ballin home and office had been in one building. The desk on which Albert had done his homework, next to his father, became covered now with business papers as the son carried on the agency—and more than carried it on.

The larger German lines had their own booking services. Most of the emigrants who came to the Ballin agency were booked on the American Line, a Philadelphia-based company operating between Liverpool and Philadelphia and New York. Though the company had an office in Liverpool, it had none in Germany, and that was where Ballin came in. He made frequent trips to Liverpool, becoming fluent in English as he cultivated the British representatives of the American Line. The studious, shy lad with the cello had grown into a bit of a hustler.

Between 1875, the year Albert entered the business, and 1881, the number of emigrants who passed through Hamburg bound for the United States rose from 25,000 to 123,000. The young entrepreneur, barely in his twenties, found his business booming. But he was growing tired of splitting commissions with Liverpool representatives of the American Line, and it was apparent that emigrants preferred direct passage to the United States. So he looked about for a local shipowner who might enable him to transport emigrants directly from Hamburg to the United States. At last, Ballin persuaded a small Hamburg freighter operator, the Carr Line, to enter passenger service. The line outfitted two freighters named *America* and *Australia* with upper-deck dormitories that provided space for 650 to 700 emigrants in each vessel. In his first year, Ballin delivered 4,000 passengers. The following year—with the addition of four modified freighters—the number almost tripled to 11,000, then rose in 1883 to 16,000.

Before long, the tiny Carr Line was giving the giant Hamburg-American Line—which was known in its homeland as HAPAG, from the initials of Hamburg-Amerikanische Packetfahrt-Actien-Gesellschaft—a run for the emigrants' money. Goliath, as one observer put it, decided to buy out David rather than fight him. In 1886 the Carr Line merged with HAPAG, and at the age of 28, Ballin became head of the big company's North American passenger service division. Now Ballin had the instru-

Set off against a backdrop of flowers and potted palms, a heroic bronze bust of Kaiser Wilhelm II, complete with imperial scepter and eagle-topped helmet, stares out across the Vaterland's elegant Social Hall. The Kaiser was such an enthusiastic supporter of the spectacular German liners, wrote a contemporary chronicler, "one would have believed that he himself had been one of the greatest factors in their success."

The winner by a beak

In the spring of 1912, soon after the Hamburg-American Line announced its launch date for the 909-foot *Imperator*, predecessor to the *Vaterland* and the largest ship ever built up to that time, the rival Cunard Line intimated that its forthcoming *Aquitania* would be longer by one foot. There was consternation in Hamburg.

Some time afterward an enormous crate arrived at the *Imperator*'s fitting-out dock. In it was a colossal gilded-bronze eagle, wings spread back and neck thrust forward, straining for every inch. On its head sat a replica of Germany's imperial crown, and in its talons it clutched a cast-iron globe. With the scowling figurehead bolted onto its prow the *Imperator* measured 919 feet from beak to stern, nine feet longer than the *Aquitania*.

The triumph was short-lived. Three voyages later, the ever-humbling Atlantic sent a mammoth wave rolling across the bows of the *Imperator* and washed the eagle's wings away. The remainder of the bird was scrapped shortly thereafter.

The Imperator's figurehead eagle, a last-minute gambit in a contest for length, adds its cumbersome bulk to the ship's prow.

ments—the men, the skills and the money—to match his own ambition.

In his first year he persuaded HAPAG to order two new liners with twin screws, an innovation that allowed the steamship, at last, to do without sail auxiliary. If one propeller shaft broke, the second propeller could bring the ship home. With the elimination of sail, the silhouette of the modern liner emerged. As form gave way to function, the bowsprit was removed and the gracefully curving clipper bows were chopped straight to present a knife-edge to the waves. Tiered superstructures and tall smokestacks rose from the hull, an impossibility so long as the masts had to support working sails. Liners still had masts, but now they were used for lights, bells, foghorns, flags and radio aerials. Ballin's new ships were pioneers in other ways. Electric lights were provided to steerage passengers, and there were even a few single-berth cabins, an unheard-of luxury in the emigrant trade.

What is more, Ballin accomplished all this with great economy. In order to get the best design at the lowest bid, he developed a policy of playing off one shipyard against another, even to the point of provoking a national rivalry. A favored foreign shipyard was the Scotch Laird yard at Birkenhead. But Ballin was a diplomat as well as an entrepreneur; the Laird yard built the *Columbia*, second of Ballin's two new liners. The first, the *Auguste Victoria*, was not only built in Germany but named after the wife of Kaiser Wilhelm II, a calculated circumstance that endeared Ballin to the Kaiser and led to a lasting friendship.

Heretofore, Ballin had been concentrating mainly on building up emigrant business. But now he turned his energies and imagination to making a name for HAPAG as a purveyor of splendid first-class service. The *Columbia* and *Auguste Victoria* had space for 580 steerage passengers, but there were also sumptuous accommodations for 400 first-class travelers. The *Auguste Victoria*'s dining room extended through two decks, and passengers descended on a rococo staircase illuminated by starlike lights held by gilded cherubs. There was a separate music room, even a separate sitting room for the ladies. On the *Auguste Victoria*'s first voyage to New York, she was visited by 30,000 people who, according to a HAPAG brochure, "expressed their admiration of her beautiful appointments in unmeasured terms."

What to do with these magnificent vessels when winter put the Elbe in ice pack and the port of Hamburg was frequently shut down? The canny Ballin, in effect, invented the first winter cruise, sending his ships from November through March on voyages into the Mediterranean and even to the Far East, where HAPAG freighters as well were industriously claiming their share of the China trade.

In 1899 Ballin was appointed managing director of HAPAG. When he had joined the firm 13 years before, the Hamburg-American Line stood 22nd among shipping lines of the world. By the turn of the century, HAPAG was well on its way to becoming the world's biggest shipping line—bigger at its peak in 1914 than the entire merchant marine of any other continental European nation. Not since Samuel Cunard himself had any one man been so responsible for the prosperity of any one line.

Ballin would rank as one of the great maritime successes if he had accomplished nothing more. He lived with his wife and adopted daugh-

ter in a large, sumptuously furnished mansion that a jealous millionaire described as a *palazzo*. Ballin was "something less than handsome," as a German diplomat tactfully put it. A more outspoken acquaintance said the Ballin face looked as if it were "formed of rubber, so that on first appearance it had an almost comic effect." The head was large and balding, with a dark fringe of tight curls. A bulbous nose surmounted a full, rather frowzy moustache, which served to disguise puffy lips. The eyes, however, were "piercing, passionate," and the voice was resonant and melodious. Ballin was a witty conversationalist, capable of talking spiritedly on any subject, and quick to sense the mood of others. He loved to entertain and was an excellent host. With the rise of HAPAG, the Kaiser himself became a dinner guest, perhaps half-a-dozen times a year.

Ballin's office, overlooking the Hamburg docks, came to reflect its master's growing prominence. Portraits of friends and associates lined the walls, and souvenirs of trips around the world decorated the tables; fresh-cut flowers were delivered every day. And there, immaculately groomed, dressed in flawless if conservative taste, Ballin operated with a certain royal flair, yet making sure, as always, to attend as well to the smallest detail—such as the plumpness of the pillows.

Albert Ballin possessed an almost superstitious sense of destiny, and he had timed things magically right. He had come to the business during the years when the transatlantic steamship was turning into the full glory of the great liner, and a shipping magnate could stand equal with other princes of finance, hobnob with real princes, and even become a friend of the Kaiser. Furthermore, he had timed his rise to coincide with the rise of Germany as a power. The *Vaterland* was to be not only Ballin's masterpiece but a symbol of Germany's might and her absolute resolution to use that strength peacefully.

For five years Ballin had been employing his considerable influence to cool the increasingly heated naval race between Germany and Britain, fueled on the one side by Admiral Alfred von Tirpitz and on the other by the young and brash Winston Churchill, who became First Lord of the Admiralty in 1911. Let the duel go on, but not between dreadnoughts, Ballin argued passionately. Let it be between the *Aquitanias* of the Cunard Line and the *Vaterlands* of his HAPAG.

On that April day, when three panting tugs guided Ballin's and Germany's new triumph to the safety of her fitting-out berth, the *Vaterland* seemed to be a sublimely blessed vessel, offered up to the sea with as much forethought as any ship ever launched. Unfortunately, Ballin's masterpiece, a ship conceived for a world of peace, was being launched into a world scarcely a year away from war.

No ship ever embodied more heroically all the aspirations that went

Shepherded by tugs and attended by a flotilla of excursion boats, the Vaterland eases out of Hamburg harbor for the first time on April 25, 1914. A few days later, during her sea trials off Norway, she achieved a top speed of 26.3 knots, almost three knots faster than that of the Aquitania, newest of the Cunarders.

Steerage: a wretched ride to America

When Robert Louis Stevenson traveled to New York aboard the Anchor Line's *Devonia* in 1879 he noted a distinction that the shipping company made between passengers. "In steerage there are males and females," he wrote. But in second cabin (and naturally in first), passengers were regarded as "ladies and gentlemen."

In the world of great liners, the ladies and gentlemen took up most of the space and enjoyed all the luxury. The steerage passengers were jammed together like so much cargo down below, and there were as many as five of them for every one affluent enough to occupy upper-class staterooms.

Virtually all of those traveling steerage were emigrants. In 1913 no fewer than 1,414,000 of them voyaged to the North American continent, and by the time immigration was restricted in the early 1920s, 30 million people had crossed steerage. The prices they paid —$50 in 1910—were a pittance compared with the $4,000 cost of a luxury suite. But they represented one third of the revenues of the shipping companies, and accounted for more than half the profits.

In the early days the overcrowded and unsanitary conditions were so bad that mortality rates reached 10 per cent some years. The British government did order improvements in the 1870s, but even then many liners had only two toilets for every 100 passengers, and the four-tiered bunks were a scant 18 inches wide.

After the turn of the century, conditions improved on some vessels, notably those of Germany. Steerage on the *Vaterland* boasted its own kitchen and dining area where stewards served three plain meals a day. But on most vessels, steerage remained, according to a Congressional report, a noisome place where "everything was dirty, every impression offensive."

A great change took place after the wave of emigrants subsided. The lower compartments were refurbished to hold fewer passengers in at least a modicum of comfort. The hateful word steerage became third class or tourist, and the new passengers were from the growing middle class of Americans who were vacationing abroad. Yet the lower decks remained a world away from first class. In 1935 the writer Ludwig Bemelmans traveled third-class on board the *Normandie* for the experience. He objected to the vibration and pitching—and even more so to "a man who had dirty finger-nails" who sat with him at table.

Their faces registering emotions from ecstasy to apprehension, emigrants on a steamer crowd every inch of the deck for their first glimpse of the promised land. Brokers who contracted for steerage space often oversold it. "We were huddled together in the steerage literally like cattle," remembered one traveler.

TABLE Showing the Number of Cabin and Steerage Passengers Landed at Port of New York during the year 1913 by the following Steamship Lines.

NAME OF STEAMSHIP LINE	WHERE FROM	AGENTS	CABIN 1st	CABIN 2nd	STEERAGE	TRIPS
NORTH GERMAN LLOYD	BREMEN	Oelrichs & Co.	16,268	28,311	131,081	126
HAMBURG AMERICAN LINE	HAMBURG	Karl Buenz	13,308	26,827	122,802	87
RED STAR LINE	ANTWERP	Red Star Line	3,074	16,625	70,051	59
FRENCH LINE	HAVRE	Paul Faguet	5,248	20,987	65,013	106
HOLLAND AMERICA LINE	ROTTERDAM	W. van Doorn } M'grs W. S. Piek	5,325	15,225	49,197	49
CUNARD STEAMSHIP CO., Limited	LIVERPOOL	Charles P. Sumner	12,991	17,127	47,300	55
CUNARD STEAMSHIP CO., Limited	FIUME	Charles P. Sumner	2,089	7,342	37,227	32
FABRE LINE	MEDITERRANEAN	James W. Elwell & Co.	1,037	3,208	36,762	45
AUSTRO Americana S.S. Co., Limited	TRIESTE	Phelps Bros. & Co.	1,235	7,470	33,923	38
NORTH GERMAN LLOYD	MEDITERRANEAN	Oelrichs & Co.	2,080	6,789	33,452	21
Navigazione Generale Italiana	MEDITERRANEAN	Hartfield, Solari & Co.	382	2,486	29,826	17
WHITE STAR LINE	LIVERPOOL	White Star Line	6,237	13,114	29,145	47
SICULA AMERICANA	MEDITERRANEAN	Peirce Brothers, Inc.	82	1,163	27,657	16
LLOYD ITALIANO	MEDITERRANEAN	C. B. Richard & Co.	1,022	1,091	26,073	18
RUSSIAN AMERICAN LINE	LIBAU	A. E. Johnson & Co. G'l Pgr. Agt.	291	5,175	23,171	29
Russian East Asiatic Steamship Co., Limited						
WHITE STAR LINE	SOUTHAMPTON	White Star Line	7,770	10,262	23,015	42
LA VELOCE	MEDITERRANEAN	Hartfield, Solari & Co.	104	1,763	21,011	11
LLOYD SABAUDO	MEDITERRANEAN	Cesare Conti	1,268	.....	19,761	14
AMERICAN LINE	SOUTHAMPTON	American Line	2,013	6,659	17,996	40
ANCHOR LINE	GLASGOW	Henderson Bros.	2,865	13,971	16,184	49
HAMBURG AMERICAN LINE	MEDITERRANEAN	Karl Buenz	1,160	4,809	16,028	16
ANCHOR LINE	MEDITERRANEAN	Henderson Bros.	144	.....	15,419	19
SCANDINAVIAN AMERICAN LINE	COPENHAGEN	A. E. Johnson & Co. G'l Pgr. Agt.	1,118	4,278	13,959	31
Italia Società Di Navigazione a Vapore	MEDITERRANEAN	Hartfield, Solari & Co.	111	923	12,846	12
URANIUM STEAMSHIP CO., Limited	ROTTERDAM	Paul G. Fourman, Pass. Agt.	51	702	10,381	22
WHITE STAR LINE	MEDITERRANEAN	White Star Line	582	1,503	6,471	5
Hellenic Trans. Steam Nav. Co., Ltd.	MEDITERRANEAN	N. A. Galanos	444	991	3,805	7
LAMPORT & HOLT LINE	SOUTH AMERICA	Busk & Daniels	2,152	1,306	3,733	41
National Steam Nav. Co., Ltd. of Greece	MEDITERRANEAN	M. Litsas	196	561	2,572	5
NORWEGIAN AMERICA LINE, Inc.	CHRISTIANIA	Norwegian America Line Passenger Agency, Inc.	217	1,117	2,521	8
COMPANIA TRANSATLANTICA	MEDITERRANEAN	J. Zaragoza	533	464	1,956	12
CUNARD STEAMSHIP CO., Limited	HAVRE	Charles P. Sumner	.....	.....	764	1
ATLANTIC TRANSPORT LINE	LONDON	Atlantic Transport Line	3,864	....	235	49
MISCELLANEOUS			56,819	8,155	4,017	1,162
			152,416	230,437	955,363	2,294

ELLIS ISLAND, January 1st, 1914.

WM. C. MOORE,
Landing Agent.

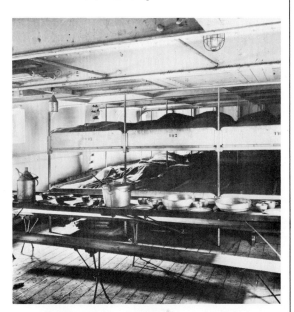

Steerage aboard the French Line's Provence around 1906 offered crowded but clean sleeping and dining facilities in one room. In the past, passengers had brought their own eating utensils and straw mattresses for the canvas berths, but the lines now provided these essentials.

This chart, which matches booking agents and embarkation points to the number of trips made by major steamship companies in 1913, shows the huge ratio of steerage passengers to those who traveled first- or second-class. Interestingly, one Cunard ship sailed from Le Havre with an all-steerage load, a special crossing probably made to meet demand in a year that registered a record 1.4 million immigrants to the U.S.

Wrapped in heavy woolen blankets and shawls, emigrant families on board the Belgian Red Star Line's Westernland in 1890 idly pass a cold day on the steerage promenade, a dreary deck used for freight handling in port. "A more forlorn party, in more dismal circumstances it would be hard to imagine," wrote Robert Louis Stevenson after observing life in steerage on an Atlantic crossing.

into a great liner; no ship ever was to suffer more embarrassments, more agonies as a consequence. Conceived as the epitome of grandeur, she sailed into a world in which grandeur, under the guns of World War I, suddenly went out of style. She was destined to become a kind of orphan wherever she sailed. Even the Atlantic would pound her as it had pounded few ships. But while the *Vaterland* prepared for her maiden voyage, such misfortune was still as remote as the adult's fate is to the child.

In the months that followed her launching, the *Vaterland* was filled in, like a rough sketch drawn to completion. The superstructure was finished—the three 64-foot smokestacks and 200-foot foremast and mainmast were erected. The great searchlight, wrapped in canvas, was mounted on the foremast. The pilothouse and the bridge were constructed of stained and varnished mahogany. The great ship took on her silhouette, her texture and coloring.

The last vital parts were added. The *Vaterland* went into dry dock—or rather docks, for two ordinary dry docks had to be joined together to contain her. Here her propellers and 50 ½-ton rudder were installed, as well as the three bow anchors. The bow ornamentation was marked in white chalk, then riveted to the hull plates: a white-and-gold shield featuring an imperial German eagle.

A new ship ceases to be the sum of her statistics only when she is inhabited: fleshed out by the voices, the footsteps—the possessiveness— of a crew. The *Vaterland*'s crew shipped aboard in proportions suitable to her size. The new Cunarder, the *Aquitania*, would boast 970 in her company. The *Vaterland* crew numbered 1,234, including an engine-room black gang of 403 and the 60 chefs, bakers and underchefs assigned to her eight kitchens.

The *Vaterland* was turning, like every ship, into a living entity with her own personality—as big, hearty and prodigal as the grandest German hotel of the day. To provision her properly, the crew carried over the side 13,800 table napkins, 6,870 tablecloths and the food to go with them: 45,000 pounds of fresh meat and 24,000 pounds of canned and pickled meats; 100,000 pounds of potatoes; 10,000 pounds of sugar, treacle and honey; and 17,500 bottles of wines, champagnes and brandies—not counting 28,000 liters of good German beer.

At last the *Vaterland* was ready to sail. Her master, Commodore Hans Ruser, remarked on May 14, 1914, the morning of her maiden voyage, "I will just point the *Vaterland* toward America and let the ocean blow by." A crowd of emigrants, shawls and caps protecting them from the drizzle, lined the rails and perched atop lifeboats on the forward deckhouse to wave farewell to friends. The departure at 2 p.m. was so quiet a maneuver that many of the first-class passengers, consuming a late luncheon in the dining saloon, were not even aware they were under way.

All told, there were 1,600 passengers on board, less than half her 4,050 capacity. But no one was overly concerned; for some reason, possibly anxiety over a new ship on the cruel sea, people had a tendency to shy away from maiden voyages.

As the *Vaterland* passed the lightship off the Isle of Wight in the English Channel, she was sighted by the *St. Louis*, the flagship of the

Dressed in evening clothes and settled in high-backed chairs drawn up to a glowing hearth, this genteel group might be taking their ease in a Bavarian Schloss instead of on board the Vaterland. With its oaken wainscoting, beamed ceiling and hanging brass lanterns, the smoking room on this liner was the epitome of Germanic rustic style.

American Line. The *St. Louis'* first mate, Herbert Hartley, recalled his first impression: "Far ahead off the starboard bow a streak of smoke showed over the horizon. I raised my binoculars. What I saw was enough to take the wind out of any sailor's canvas. There she stood out to sea, her three great funnels towering proudly above her upper deck. I didn't say a word. I just stood there and looked. She was the biggest ship that had ever sailed the seas."

"Sir," Hartley said to his skipper, Captain John Clark Jamison, "the captain of that ship must indeed be a proud man."

Captain Jamison tugged his goatee, shifted his pipe and spat to leeward. After an appropriate pause, he growled: "Let him try to get up the English Channel some dirty night when he doesn't know where he is and he won't feel so damn proud."

Years later, Hartley would have a chance to know, firsthand, how it felt: one day he would become captain of that ship.

The maiden voyage, for the superstitious, is an omen. In that respect, the *Vaterland* appeared blessed. Everything worked. At night the 15,000 electric lights went on all over the ship. When it turned cool, the heating units quickly warmed the cabins. Oxygen was pumped into the smoking room each morning, clearing the tobacco smog of the previous day. The

palm trees flourished in the Palm Court. The greenhouse on the upper deck prolifically produced flowers to grace tables in the Ritz-Carlton Restaurant (an exact copy of the New York Ritz), where just the cold-cuts menu included pork chops in jelly, duck à la Montmorency, beefsteak tartare, roast beef, roast veal, smoked ox tongue, ham and uncounted varieties of sausage.

Everything seemed to function properly, even the stream of water a winged, unclad youth on a marble column sent arching into the Pompeian swimming pool. Athletic passengers splashed at water polo, then climbed to an upper deck to tango to the ship's orchestra, or simply absorb the splendor on view. In the 75-foot Social Hall hung four oils, each 13 feet high and 12 feet wide, depicting the legend of Pandora. The work of a 17th Century Flemish artist, the paintings had been presented to the ship by the Kaiser from his private collection, along with Houdon's bronze statue of Marie Antoinette—and, naturally, a bust of the German ruler himself. Exhausted by the rigors of polo, tango or *Kultur*, a gentleman could retreat to the barbershop, close his eyes and have his mustache curled for 10 cents.

Had the Atlantic ever been so suavely conquered? A comment of a *Vaterland* junior officer only slightly overstated the mood. One viewed,

A bevy of Germanic beauties, artistically arranged by the cameraman, adorns the Vaterland's indoor Pompeian-style "swimming bath." The pool extended through three decks with 69 square yards of swimming space and a maximum depth of eight feet. That was nothing, of course, compared with the splash the Normandie would make with her pool and other luxuries in the 1930s (pages 80-89).

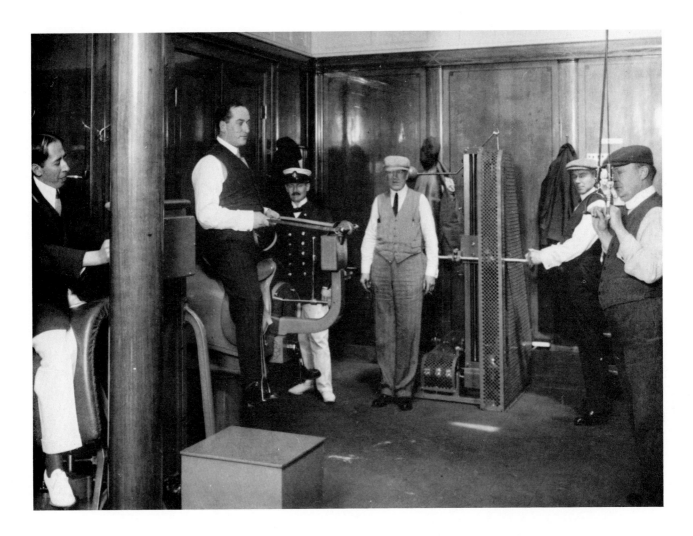

Exercising in the wood-paneled, skylighted gymnasium of the Vaterland is clearly a not-too-strenuous activity for these inappropriately attired passengers in first class, as they gingerly tug at weights and sit astride mechanical horses. Passengers in the liner's second class had their own gymnasium, but alas, it offered them only such mundane pieces of equipment as weights.

he said, "as though from Olympus, the awesome spectacle of the monstrous ship thrusting her knifelike bow into the relentless Atlantic." Then, almost at the last minute, this young ocean tamer was humiliated.

On the morning of May 21, 1914, the largest crowd ever to see a new ship arrive in New York Harbor gathered at pierside (actually in Hoboken, New Jersey, across the river from Manhattan), lured by four-column headlines in the *New York World:* "$6,000,000 Sea Monster *Vaterland* to Move Majestically into This Harbor Today."

The sun was shining, and the triumphal scene could not have proceeded more smashingly. Then suddenly, just as the *Vaterland* was about to nose into her pier, a small tug laboring upstream with a tow of barges blundered across the great liner's bow. In alarm, the pilot who was docking her gave the order to stop all engines; the *Vaterland* hung dead in the water. Within a few minutes, the intruding tug and her barges had struggled out of the way.

Then an awful thing happened. This ship of ships, longer than the tallest building in the world was tall—the Woolworth Building, off to starboard—suddenly turned into a paralyzed giant. Each one of her 46 boilers was capable of more than 1,300 horsepower. And yet at this moment, just past 9:30 a.m., the *Vaterland* was helpless: a 950-foot steel

How big? So big!

Words could evoke the ambiance of a great liner. To say a saloon resembled an alpine *Schloss* or a Mayfair club was to conjure up images of Bavarian *Gemütlichkeit* or Edwardian elegance.

But how to convey the liner's immensity? When words failed, publicists superimposed the liners on well-known buildings or showed railroad trains chuffing through their funnels. And the greater the liner the greater the possibilities, as shown by the items here from a 1908 Cunard pamphlet entitled "*Lusitania and Mauretania—Some Interesting Comparisons.*"

From Cunard's promotion pamphlet on the 32,000-ton sister ships Mauretania and Lusitania, this drawing graphically illustrates the 900-man crew necessary to operate a grand hotel afloat.

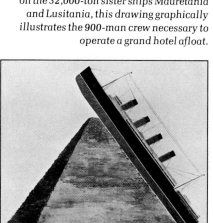

Egypt's Great Pyramid is dwarfed by the mighty Mauretania, but then, as the booklet clearly illustrated, so was the U.S. Capitol in Washington, as well as St. Peter's and the Vatican in Rome. For the British, the Cunard Line compared its vessels (favorably) with the Caledonian Railway Bridge in Glasgow and, of course, the Houses of Parliament in London.

Just the entrees for a transatlantic voyage were enough to stock a lordly estate, as the teeming acreage above indicates. Another drawing showed a dock laden with all of the necessary turbot, sole, herring (both kippered and red), salmon, haddock, ling, oysters and bloaters. For those favoring turtle soup there were three of the beasts—325 pounds in all.

Her props projecting like gigantic clovers, the Mauretania rests uncomfortably in Northumberland Avenue, opening off London's Trafalgar Square. Cunard carefully explained that "this well-known avenue is 84 feet wide, four feet less than the beam of the Mauretania, so that the buildings on either side would be completely wrecked were the ship placed in this important London artery."

Just to fuel the Mauretania or Lusitania on a voyage between Liverpool and New York, Cunard computed, would require "22 coal trains of 30 trucks, each truck containing 10 tons"—and that, as any reader could plainly see, was a veritable railway yard of coal.

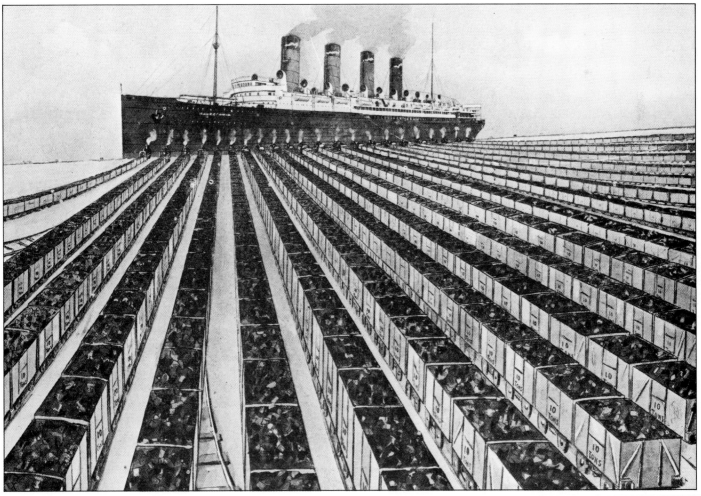

sail blown broadside by a gusty wind and both the current and the tide. She began to move inexorably downstream. The pilot ordered renewed power from her engines, but there was no space to maneuver. Fourteen tugs, like Lilliputians, frantically pulled and shoved at her inert body: five hauled with hawsers at the bow, three nudged the starboard side and six strained at the port. Still the *Vaterland* continued her slow drift toward a mudbank by the Lackawanna ferry channel, where the deepest sounding was 27 feet, 10 feet too shallow to accommodate her draft. More and more tugs swarmed to the rescue—25 according to *The New York Times,* 50 according to less conservative counts.

Finally all that mass was halted in its downstream course, just short of the mudbank. The incoming tide arrived to help provide headway, and at 12:15, almost three hours late, the *Vaterland* was again ready for docking. It required another hour to make her fast—her stern extending into the Hudson 25 feet past her berth. The New York papers were agog. "The Hamburg leviathan had the longest and hardest docking in fair weather the port ever saw," said the *New York Herald.* "The *Vaterland,* an unhappy bumbler from the start," commented a less kind chronicler.

The *Vaterland*'s departure was scarcely less eventful. At 10 a.m. just five days later, her harbor pilot apparently miscalculated the power of her engines and backed her out of her Hoboken slip with a mad burst of speed. The *Vaterland*'s momentum carried her clear across the Hudson—until she came ingloriously to rest in the mud between piers 50 and 51 at the foot of Jane Street in Greenwich Village. Now the panicky pilot compounded the situation by calling for too much power ahead. When the *Vaterland*'s props began threshing like the flukes of a beached whale, two small steamers nearby were sucked from their berths, hawsers snapping like a cannon shot. In the backwash the steamers were thrown against their piers, shattering bulkheads, rails and stanchions. A barge just offshore, carrying almost 800 tons of coal, was swamped in the maelstrom created by the *Vaterland*'s props. The barge captain survived by jumping to the pier, but an engineer on board a nearby railroad tug was not so fortunate; as his craft wallowed in the *Vaterland*'s waves, he fell overboard and drowned.

Incredible as it may seem, none of this appears to have made much impression upon the men high above on the *Vaterland*'s bridge. It was as if the *Vaterland* had rendered them blindly oblivious to anything not on her scale. As the gigantic props freed her from the muck, the *Vaterland* moved out to midriver, turned and steamed away.

The *Vaterland* had shown her particular vulnerability. All her life she was to be out of size for the world she inhabited, and curiously out of phase as well—both ahead of her times and behind them. Despite all her breathtaking boldness, all her specific ingenuities of design, there was something 19th Century, something quaintly Jules Verne about Albert Ballin's dream. It was a futuristic vision that had come too late.

Ballin may have sensed it. He had built his great liner as the ultimate expression of a nation, a world, at peace. Now his health, never the best, deteriorated as the omens of war became more and more manifest. Overworked and nervous, he was tormented by insomnia and depended on sleeping pills. His outbursts of temper—sudden, terrifying—became more frequent. He vacillated between his old mountaintop optimism and new depths of despondency. On his desk he placed the framed motto: "Life is just one damn thing after another." In despair he wrote to a friend: "Nothing to be done against the forces that are at work. One can only be resigned to watch the development of this frightful experience. I am seized by a deep melancholy from which I cannot deliver myself."

Within three months of the *Vaterland*'s maiden voyage, World War I broke out. Ballin's premonitions were justified. On July 22, 1914, the great vessel set out on a westbound crossing. On July 28, when she was two days out of New York, Austria-Hungary declared war on tiny Serbia.

On July 31 the *Vaterland* had her steam up, preparing to depart New York for a return to Hamburg. Baggage was aboard, being distributed to cabins. More than $225,000 had been collected from 2,700 passengers. Then a cable arrived from Germany, warning that British and French cruisers were lying in ambush off New York, waiting to seize the *Vaterland* if she sailed. The voyage was canceled. The *Vaterland* was to remain at Hoboken, pending further instructions.

On August 3 Germany declared war on France, and the following day Great Britain declared war on Germany. In the first hot breath of hysteria, a New York City police launch with an enormous searchlight was sent to keep an eye on this vessel belonging to a belligerent. Though the United States was officially neutral, the press was very much pro-Ally; the papers were full of stories that the *Vaterland* was prepared to make a run for it under cover of darkness and—marvelous to tell—that she would then be converted into a cruiser while on the high seas. The *New York Tribune* went so far as to report breathlessly that the *Vaterland* would be taking with her 8,000 to 10,000 German sympathizers who had somehow gone aboard, willing to go to war for the fatherland.

In fact, the *Vaterland* was as effectively trapped as if in a tomb. Built to survive a thousand Atlantic crossings, she had completed just seven. The irony was that the last six trips had been smooth to the point of happy uneventfulness. Business was more than satisfactory. On her second eastbound voyage, 3,151 passengers had sailed.

Next to sinking, the most degrading fate that can befall a ship is stagnation. Tied to a pier, motionless except for the ebb and flow of the tide or the passing wake of an active ship, the idle vessel lives only in the process of disintegration—in the rust that forms, in the marine life that silently attacks it. The greater the ship, the greater the deterioration. The *Vaterland* was the greatest ship in the world and she was chained to a dock in Hoboken, immobilized before her life had fairly begun by "this insane war," as the infuriated Ballin called it.

How the man who had conceived the *Vaterland* suffered. With a kind of desperate reasonableness, Ballin proposed neutralizing the *Vaterland*—using her as a peace ship, transporting relief supplies to Belgium. Herbert Hoover, establishing his reputation as a tireless worker for the Belgian Relief Commission in Europe, agreed with Ballin. The German Admiralty did not.

And so the months went by. She was not officially interned; she was still awaiting orders. More than half her crew refused the chance to return home. Day and night, they loyally stood regular watches (at reduced pay). During their spare time they ice-skated on the frozen Hudson in winter and dived, nude, into the murky river in the summer. Once the initial hysteria had subsided, they hung around German-American haunts in Hoboken. The *Vaterland* band played jolly shoreside concerts in order to raise funds for the German relief effort, and such Anglophobes as William Randolph Hearst attended charity balls on board and donated generously.

But after the British Cunarder *Lusitania* was sunk by a German U-boat on May 7, 1915 *(pages 136-137)*, the atmosphere changed. *The New York Times* suggested seizing German liners in reprisal. The German sympathizers who swarmed up the gangplank to attend parties, splashing equally in the swimming pool and the wine cellar, suddenly looked treacherous to many New Yorkers. Rumors began to hum again that the *Vaterland* was going to make a run for it, that Commodore Ruser and the crew were sabotaging her, or even preparing to blow her up. Now the *Vaterland* was in a state of psychological siege. As time crept by, large numbers of disheartened seamen accepted the United States offer of passage home. By the spring of 1917, only about 300 of the ship's original complement of 1,200 crewmen remained on board.

The *Vaterland* had spent almost three of the first four years of her existence in limbo, waiting for whatever the fates might have in store. It was almost a relief to Commodore Ruser and the weary remnant of his crew when the issue was finally decided just as he had suspected all along it would be.

Shackled giants, eight German liners, including the colossal Vaterland at far left, lie tied up at Hoboken, New Jersey, where they sought refuge from enemy warships at the outbreak of World War I. When the United States entered the War 32 months later, the 35 German ships in American ports were seized by the government; many were put into service as troop transports and hospital ships, and after the War ended, were converted back to liners under the U.S. flag.

The night of Thursday, April 5, 1917, was "a vicious bitchy night," John Baylis recalled; "it was raining like the devil." A Treasury officer, Baylis led a task force of 200 soldiers in an amphibious operation of comic-opera overkill against the *Vaterland*. The United States government had at last decided to seize the vessel. Although the United States was not yet officially at war, it might as well have been. On January 31 the Germans had announced a policy of unrestricted submarine warfare; on February 3 the United States had broken off diplomatic relations; and from that point on, German U-boats had been aggressively attacking American merchant shipping.

At 4 a.m. on April 6, Baylis and his men embarked in four New York police harbor-patrol launches and motored across the Hudson River to Hoboken. Disembarking on the pier where the *Vaterland* had been moored for such a long time, Baylis observed that "every column seemed to have a Customs man behind it, for the pier had been under close Treasury Department surveillance for some time." Here was the still-majestic ship, and here was all this slightly silly sneaking about. As Baylis and his men swarmed self-consciously up the gangplank to take control, from the bridge of the *Vaterland* a voice rang out loud and clear: "I protest." Then it was all over.

The 300 or so crew members of the *Vaterland* were taken to Ellis Island and questioned. After medical examinations they were rather astonishingly invited to take out first citizenship papers and enter the United States as immigrants. About 250 of them (not including Commodore Ruser) accepted. At 1:13 p.m., less than 10 hours after the occupation of

the *Vaterland,* the United States declared war on Germany. Ruser and 49 officers and seamen ended up in Hot Springs, North Carolina, detained for the duration in the Mountain Park Hotel. The war was over for them. It had just begun for their ship.

Most ships, like most human beings, go through life with one identity— performing one function, belonging to one nation, answering to one name. The *Vaterland,* the greatest of her generation's great liners, became a troop transport for the fatherland's enemy. She was renamed the *Leviathan* by the American President, Woodrow Wilson, who without even raising his eyes from his papers in the White House, suggested: "*Leviathan.* It's in the Bible, monster of the deep."

A new name for the ship was the simple part. When United States Navy men first climbed aboard, they were appalled at her condition. "You will never run her," Chief Engineer Otto Wolf had snapped as he stepped off the ship on his way to Ellis Island. The words haunted the Navy and civilian engineers who teamed together to put the *Leviathan* in working order. There were fears of booby traps. "We were opening and closing doors and we did not know what minute, while groping in the dark with searchlights, something was going to happen to us," a Navy engineer recalled.

There were no explosives, but there had been some sabotage. A number of piston and connecting rods had been cut. The engine-room telegraph had been smashed. Steam lines had been disjointed, plugged with brass, then rejoined again. Threads on bolts had been filed almost smooth so that they would give way under pressure.

But far more damage had occurred from simple neglect than from deliberate abuse. There were leaking tubes in all of the ship's 46 boilers. The astern turbines needed new blades—38,000 of them—and the Coe Brass Works of New Britain, Connecticut, closed down its regular production lines for two weeks in order to make the necessary replacements. The German operators had removed all of the instruction books and wiring diagrams from the radio shack. It took specialists some three months to put the Telefunken set back in working order. And so it went, all over the gigantic vessel. Miles and miles of pipes and electric wiring had to be inspected inch by inch.

In addition to mechanical restoration, there was the far less delicate job of conversion. Turning the *Leviathan* into a troopship was roughly the equivalent of converting the Ritz into army barracks. About 1,200 staterooms were ripped out and replaced by compartments with triple-tiered iron-rack bunks. Sledge hammers were used to remove bathtubs; cushions and chairs were tossed overboard; leaded-glass windows and mirrors were smashed. There was looting to match. Customhouse guards were caught guzzling rare Moselle. Paintings were mutilated, first and foremost a portrait of Ludwig of Bavaria, whom sailors mistook for the Kaiser. What was not stolen went on public auction on the pier. An electrician working on the *Leviathan* described the sad, often barbaric process as "the gutting of the German whale."

Painted Navy gray, the *Leviathan* was ready to sail on November 17, seven months after she had been seized. With memories still vivid of her

A dazzling scheme to confound U-boats

It was a metamorphosis to stagger the eye. On January 15, 1918, the *Leviathan* interrupted her wartime duty as a troop transport and went into Gladstone Dry Dock, Liverpool, for routine maintenance. When she emerged she appeared to have been the victim of an insane artist, for she was splashed from stem to stern with a bizarre pattern of multicolored squares, stripes, wedges and zigzags.

There was, of course, a method to this madness. It was intended to save the *Leviathan* from the torpedoes of prowling U-boats. "Dazzle painting," as this crazy-quilt design was called, originated with British Navy officer and marine artist Norman Wilkinson.

Wilkinson knew that against a backdrop of open sea and sky it was quite impossible to camouflage a ship so that she would be virtually invisible. He suggested the opposite extreme. By using violently contrasting bands of black, white, blue and gray paint, he sought to break the silhouette of a ship and to puzzle an enemy as to her direction of travel. The theory was that a U-boat captain would be so confused over the ship's true course, he would take up an incorrect firing position —and miss with his torpedo. Dazzle painting quickly caught on among the Allies, and in 1917 Wilkinson came to the United States to help the U.S. Navy set up its own dazzle department.

There was no way to record the effectiveness of the dazzle camouflage. But in the case of the *Leviathan*, her weird paint job was so confusing that a destroyer escort sent to accompany her out of Liverpool harbor had to circle her before its captain could be sure which way she was headed.

Hundreds of different dazzle patterns were concocted, each calculated to boggle the eye with confusing optical illusions. At right are four of the designs that were drawn up for use on four-stackers.

The Leviathan steams out of New York Harbor, resplendent in her new war paint.

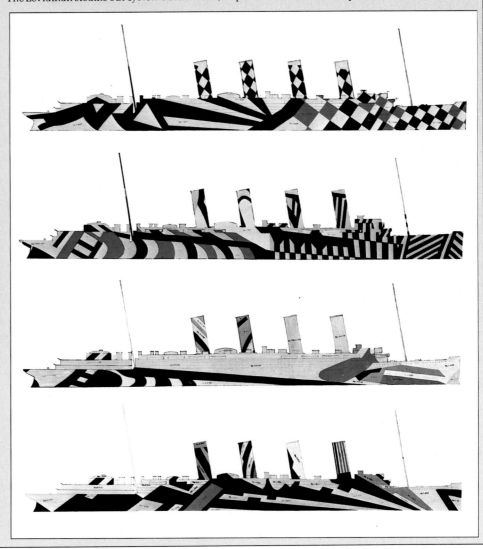

initial departure from Hoboken, the Navy laid on no fewer than 46 tugs to assist her as she cautiously backed out of her slip. Loose silt had built up 27 feet high around her keel; her giant propellers dispersed it in great rolling clouds across the river.

As a troop transport, the *Leviathan* soon proved she had lost none of her talent for the unexpected. She went aground off Liverpool. She nearly asphyxiated her crew (including a young quartermaster named Humphrey Bogart) when her ventilating system unaccountably commenced to work backward, filling the ship with engine-room fumes. She sailed in a giddy circle when a valve stem on the port steering engine broke. The *Vaterland* was equipped with two steering engines to guard against just such a contingency, and the starboard steering engine was cut in to provide control while the port engine was undergoing repairs. But it, too, soon suffered a broken valve stem—which rendered the ship truly helpless, with no steering whatsoever. The new chief engineering officer, Lieutenant Vaughn Veazey Woodward, rushed to the machine shop and, using heavier materials and a modified pattern, invented a new valve stem. It worked.

And so, in the long run, did the *Leviathan*. She made 19 round trips during the war, and on one crossing she carried 14,416 troops—more human beings than had ever before sailed on a single ship. Of the two million American troops who were transported across the Atlantic, one out of every 20 was ferried on the *Leviathan*. The doughboys had mixed feelings about "The Big Train," as they nicknamed her. Among other things, she had a long, deliberate, corkscrewing pitch and roll that could make a landlubber seasick in slow motion, as it were. The standard joke was a two-line dialogue:

"Here comes a torpedo."

"Thank God!"

On her final crossing as a troop transport, she carried 7,000 doughboys of the famed Rainbow Division and the hero of the hour, General John J. Pershing, commander of all United States forces. The Knights of Columbus had rashly promised that every soldier on board could send a free radiogram home from the ship; the men in the radio shack, laboring mightily, got out all but 1,000 of them by the time she docked in Hoboken, firing them off at the rate of almost one every minute for the duration of the voyage.

In a way, that act was symbolic of her military career. For all her foibles, she had performed heroically. And she was truly deserving of the accolade bestowed by Secretary of War Newton D. Baker, who described her as "the glory of the transport service. Where," he asked, "shall we find such a tale of cooperation, efficiency, and daring? It is a great career, worthy of the greatest ship in the world."

At last, five years after her maiden voyage, it was time for the *Leviathan* to resume her three-month career as a great liner. But the man who had conceived and built her was no longer alive to be a witness to her rebirth. Albert Ballin had taken an overdose of sleeping pills on November 9, 1918, just two days before the Armistice. It seemed unlikely that there might be anyone left in an exhausted and disillusioned world who would dream again his dream.

How to berth a behemoth

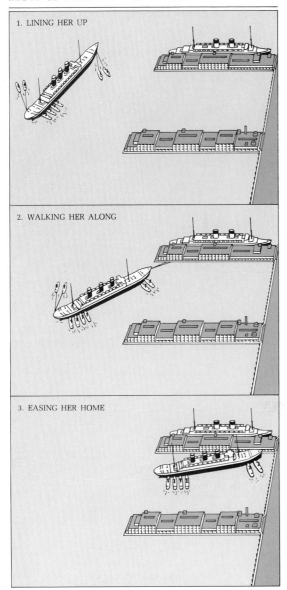

1. LINING HER UP

2. WALKING HER ALONG

3. EASING HER HOME

The pin-point maneuvering required to dock the Vaterland begins after evaluation of the wind and tide (1), with tugs pulling at the bow and pushing at the stern. As the ship's bow nears the pier (2), a heavy hawser is run from her windlass and fastened to a bollard. Aided by tugs, the ship heaves in on the hawser, pulling herself forward until another hawser can be secured to the next bollard. The liner is thus "walked along" from bollard to bollard until she is fully in her slip (3) and tugs can nudge her against the pier.

William Francis Gibbs, tall, bespectacled, aristocratic, with thin, austere lips, was studying law at Columbia when the *Leviathan* was built. From boyhood he had three passions in life—theater, fire engines and ships. The last passion conquered him, and he became a naval architect, an uncompromising perfectionist to rival Ballin.

In 1920, at the age of 33, he threw himself into redesigning the *Leviathan* as the American superliner of the coming decade, flagship of the United States Lines. When the German firm of Blohm & Voss demanded a million dollars for a set of the original blueprints, Gibbs organized a team of 100 draftsmen who walked and crawled over the ship, measuring her from scratch and making their own blueprints. The U.S. Navy had put her in working order. But there was a vast difference between the emergency needs of a transport command and the day-in, day-out requirements of a transatlantic company with regular schedules to meet.

From the point of view of the naval architect, as Gibbs explained, "there was nothing to go by but the ship herself. We knew nothing whatever about her. We did not even know where her center of gravity was." It took Gibbs and his men a solid year before they could present a set of plans to the United States Shipping Board. The specifications were as remarkable as Ballin's: 1,024 pages long, supplemented by more than 20 blueprints. Among Gibbs's recommendations was a proposal to convert the *Leviathan* to an oil burner, and her Ritz-Carlton Restaurant to electric cooking. Like Ballin, he was a stickler for details. Thirteen pages were devoted to clockface designs: clocks with sea-shell and dolphin designs, clocks with ship's bells and heaving lines and, for the children's dining saloon, a clock with a sort of nautical Santa Claus, rope entwined. The restoration, Gibbs figured, would cost about $10 million.

Gibbs was now engrossed in his ship. Others were not so certain the *Leviathan* was worth it. Giant liners like her were "no longer profitable," *The New York Times* editorialized, proposing that she "be towed up the Hudson and moored"; she might then be converted into a floating apartment that would house as many as 3,000 tenants, even with one deck partially reserved for tennis courts.

Coaxed, nagged and memoed half to death by Gibbs, the United States Shipping Board finally gave a blanket okay to his recommendations. In April 1922 the *Leviathan*—after languishing nearly three years at Hoboken—steamed to Newport News, Virginia, where she was rebuilt for over three million dollars more than it had cost to build her a decade before.

A certain obvious Americanization occurred. In the library, where the now-destroyed portrait of Ludwig of Bavaria once held the place of honor, there appeared a Howard Chandler Christy portrait of President Warren G. Harding. The ship's three huge stacks were painted red, white and blue. Gibbs changed his mind about converting all the kitchens to electric cooking (it was too expensive), but he did shift from coal to more economic oil to fuel her boilers. Forty-six tanks were installed to contain the 9,563 tons of oil the *Leviathan* would consume per crossing.

On July 4, 1923, this third version of Hull No. 212 sailed on what could be thought of as her third maiden voyage. Despite telephones in every room and the promise of pre-release motion pictures, only 1,792 passengers were on board, or a little more than half capacity. But that was still

enough to make a profit, and when the crossing went smoothly from start to finish, the omens seemed favorable at last. She returned without incident with 1,174 passengers, also at a profit.

The first three voyages of the reborn *Leviathan* were, in fact, in the black. Then she hit five straight losses, ending up with a net deficit of $70,897 for 1923. A brief 10 years after launching, Ballin's ship was sailing into a radically different world from the one for which she had been designed. Three quarters of the space on the *Vaterland* was reserved territory for the 700 first-class passengers she was prepared to accommodate. But almost five times that number—3,350—were crowded into second and third class and steerage on a full-capacity trip. The emigrant was the bread-and-butter customer on whose trade the caviar-and-champagne menus of first class depended.

But emigration declined precipitously with the establishment by the United States of strict quotas in the early 1920s. By 1924 the number of passengers sailing to the United States had dropped to 528,000—less than one third of what the figure had been before World War I. Approxi-

Wearing a coat of Navy gray and a new name—Leviathan—after her seizure by the United States and duty as a wartime troop transport, the ex-Vaterland lies at dockside in Newport News, Virginia, undergoing reconversion into a luxury liner for the U.S. Lines. Begun in 1922, the job took 2,600 workers 15 months.

mately the same number of competitors—80 lines were supplying transatlantic passenger service—fought for a drastically reduced trade.

The *Leviathan* could not compete in this fierce climate. For one thing, as an American ship she was subject to that hated bit of postwar puritanism, Prohibition. Ships flying foreign flags became floating bars, irresistibly appealing to dry-mouthed Americans.

It was not uncommon for the *Leviathan* to make a crossing with 700 or 800 passengers—considerably fewer than her complement of 1,200 in crew. To make matters worse, she was inordinately expensive to run. Despite the conversion from coal, she was a mammoth fuel guzzler, consuming $120,000 worth of oil per round trip.

Then there were the bizarre accidents that always seemed to dog the *Leviathan*. At one point she set a distance record for one day's run—625 miles—and then, approaching New York Harbor, she ran aground off Staten Island and did $250,000 damage to the pipes of a new sewer system that extended into the channel near Robbins Reef. Her captain, Herbert Hartley, who had first seen her in the English Channel in 1914, maintained: "If ever I drove a ship with caution, I drove the *Leviathan* with caution that night. Barely drifting, the liner reached Robbins Reef. From there in I would go to starboard to follow the channel lights. But she wanted to go to port. The ship won and my heart almost stopped."

Even the Atlantic seemed to have it in for this proud ship. In November 1925, more than 1,000 passengers—an unusually large number for that time of year—embarked for the westbound crossing at Southampton and Cherbourg. Mrs. Rudolph Valentino was numbered among them. So was Mrs. David Meriwether Milton, daughter of John D. Rockefeller Jr. She was on her honeymoon, and what a honeymoon it turned out to be. The second day out, in the laconic language of the log, "the ship was hove to in a whole gale from southwest by south, velocity 65 miles per hour." The battered ship rolled 15° and pitched so heavily that she took green water over her forward deck. The helmsman fought to hold a course that would catch each wave at a 45° angle. To meet the waves head on would risk breaking the ship apart; to catch a wave broadside could mean capsizing. Captain Hartley spent 72 consecutive hours on the bridge. "It was like riding a giant roller coaster," he recalled. "Much of the time my feet were washed from under me. It was only when the *Leviathan* slid down into the valleys between the mountainous waves that I was able to set my feet on solid footing. There was a lull, a poise, then it was up and over and again pounding, washing, breaking sea and I gripped the railing to cling on for life itself."

All doors to the outer decks were locked. But suddenly, just when the gale was at its worst, Captain Hartley felt a tugging at his arm. "Startled, I turned. There stood a woman, her clothes and hair drenched and dripping. 'Captain!' she yelled, 'are you afraid?' 'My God!' I bellowed, 'How did you get up here?' Pointing, she indicated the almost vertical ladder that led to the deck below. I grabbed her around the waist with one arm and said: 'I'm not afraid. This happens on every crossing.' "

With the first dip into a trough, Hartley had the woman hustled off the bridge. It took five sailors to carry her screaming to her cabin and the care of the ship's doctor—when he could be spared from tending to victims

William Francis Gibbs (right), the lawyer-turned-naval-architect who masterminded and personally directed the stupendous task of refurbishing the Leviathan after World War I, shares a moment on the ship's deck with skipper Herbert Hartley.

like the ship's carpenter, whose leg was broken by a sliding piano.

The *Leviathan* was driven 75 miles north off her course. Yet, as Hartley poured on the speed to make up the delay, she arrived in New York, her red-white-and-blue funnels caked with salt, only one day late. On her next westbound crossing, over two weeks later, the *Leviathan* averaged 24.28 knots and made the fastest passage of the year: five days, six hours and 26 minutes.

As the '20s boomed, there was hope that the *Leviathan*, though still losing money and requiring a government subsidy to operate, might eventually make it on her own. Her lists of passengers were second to none in panache. On one crossing she carried movie stars Gloria Swanson, Douglas Fairbanks and Mary Pickford; famed golfer Walter Hagen; New York's most popular minister, Dr. Harry Emerson Fosdick; the Duc and Duchesse de Richelieu; Percival S. Hill, president of the American Tobacco Company; the Maharajah Rajenda Bahadur of Jin; Mrs. Whitelaw Reid, wife of the editor and publisher of the *New York Herald Tribune*; the violinist Jascha Heifetz; and Fung Chung, Chinese Minister to the Court of St. James.

Yet of all the crossings on the *Leviathan*, none diffused more glamor than the westbound sailing of Queen Marie of Rumania in October 1926. From the moment the Queen glided up the red-carpeted gangway at Cherbourg, followed by ladies in waiting, aides-de-camp and 90 trunks, the voyage had the unreality of a movie in the making. The Queen made a point of leaving no part of the ship unvisited. Wearing a fur coat open just enough to display long chains of pearls and a large corsage, she toured the bridge with the captain, and the engine room with the chief engineer. Her Scottish terrier was savaged by a cat in the galley—one of several hundred that kept the *Leviathan* rat-free. No matter. The Queen forgave the offending creature and swept on to inspect crew quarters and steerage accommodations. She particularly sought out Rumanians in third class. At the end of the voyage, anything less than tug whistles and fireboat salutes in New York Harbor and a ticker-tape parade up Broadway would have been anticlimactic. When, at the last, Mayor Jimmy Walker hesitated as he pinned a medal on her generous bosom, the Queen said: "Proceed, Your Honor, the risk is mine."

The next year, 1927, the *Leviathan* carried a record number of passengers for a single crossing—2,741—and on this voyage, at least, she was in the black. In August of that year she played maritime pioneer when the first mailplane to be launched from a liner took off from a 100-foot ramp built on her teak bridge, pointing diagonally over the port side of the flying bridge. Clarence Chamberlin's tiny Fokker biplane was airborne within 75 feet, 80 miles east of Ambrose Light. A gesture as much as an event, the flight seemed to symbolize the anything-is-possible hope of an incredibly optimistic era. But the good times were, in fact, fast coming to a close. An event in the fateful year of 1929 symbolized the beginning of the end for the *Leviathan*. Like everything else in that ship's history, it was on a grand scale.

On the evening of December 11, 1929, the *Leviathan* was about three quarters of the way across on an eastbound passage, pounding into a heavy sea, nearing the end of what had been a two-day gale. Second

All set to take off from the Leviathan with the first ship-to-shore airmail delivery on August 1, 1927, Clarence Chamberlin warms the Wright Whirlwind engine of his Fokker biplane on a specially built, 100-foot-long ramp still wet from a passing squall. Despite threatening weather, Chamberlin took to the air and flew the 80 miles to New York in grand style.

Officer Sherman Reed, observing the obvious—that the ship was taking a beating—suggested slowing down. Her captain was now Harold Cunningham; Hartley had retired, and Cunningham, previously captain of the *George Washington*, the United States Lines' second-largest vessel, had moved up to command the flagship. He declined to cut back on full speed, remarking with the touch of jealousy captains have for predecessors: "This is not a Hartley schedule. This is a Cunningham schedule."

Cunningham and Reed were on the bridge shortly after 8:30 p.m. when Reed sighted a 40-foot wave coming at them out of the darkness and shouted the reflexive sailor's warning: "Hold on!" The wave crashed down over the bow—tons and tons of pile-driving water. There was a springing sensation as the forward half of the ship bent like a diving board, then a sharp crack ripped through the sounds of the storm.

Suddenly the *Leviathan* had an inch-wide crack on her starboard side, going down 20 feet to C deck and putting the deck frames out of true. Nearly every door in the forward crew and passenger quarters jammed.

In the morning a strange sight greeted the passengers and crew of the *Leviathan*. As the ship heaved in the heavy swells, the crack expanded and contracted; where the rivets joining the plates had popped, the rivet holes opened and shut like tiny eyes.

When the *Leviathan* reached Southampton, an emergency patch up was done by the Harland & Wolff Shipyard. Heavy I beams braced the cracked deck in alignment. On the return trip, as a precaution, the vessel followed the longer but less stormy southern route. In New York the United States Lines took her out of service to make extensive repairs. Before the job was done, 64 cabins had to be ripped out and replaced.

By late March, 1930, the *Leviathan* was as sound as ever. But the repairs had cost $700,000. And there was no way to get it back. The Great Depression had fallen on the world, and travel was a luxury only the very, very rich indulged in. There were not enough passengers for a decent captain's dinner. On one crossing the crew of 1,200 catered to but 301 passengers in all classes.

By the early 1930s the *Leviathan* was reduced to playing cruise ship between monthly Atlantic crossings. One folder, advertising a "weekend house party" to Halifax and back, invited patrons: "Come! Put a paperweight on care and sail bracing northern seas. Judge these four days on the world's most famous ship for what they are worth to you." On a cruise to nowhere over Columbus Day, 1932—three days for $35— 1,800 people were packed on board, most of them with one thing in mind. Prohibition was still in force ashore but was no longer observed on shipboard beyond United States territorial waters. A detail of seamen stood special around-the-clock watch on deck to keep the drunks from falling overboard. The bargain was too cheap. The cruise lost $14,000.

In June 1934, the *Leviathan* was overhauled for the last time. She made five round trips to Europe, all at thumping losses, the average being $60,000. At last, in September, she was returned to her own particular purgatory, Hoboken, where she collected rust for another four years.

In January 1938 the *Leviathan* sailed for the last time, on the way to her graveyard—Rosyth, Scotland, where she would be cut up into scrap. It was as dismal a day as Ballin at his gloomiest could have imagined. A smog screen hung evilly over Manhattan. The *Leviathan* was so silted up—so inseparable from the muck in which she had been resting—that fueling was postponed until she reached Staten Island lest full tanks make her immovable. She barely limped clear of the harbor before one of her boilers burst; another nine were inoperable. She began her last journey firing only 36 of her 46 boilers. Another 12 would break down in the seven days she took to cross the Atlantic.

Having flown the German flag as the *Vaterland* and the American flag as the *Leviathan*, the dying ship now showed a third flag, the red duster of the British merchant marine, in recognition of her last ragtag crew. An English sea dog named J. M. Binks was summoned from retirement to be final skipper to Ballin's 24-year-old dream. On his last previous assignment, as captain of the old *Olympic*, Binks had sliced the Nantucket Lightship in two on a foggy May morning in 1934. Seven of the lightship's crew had died. Retirement to a cottage in Lancashire suited Binks. He was not the luckiest of men. And now he had a ship to match him.

There was a leak aft that the pumps could not contain, and only by shifting fuel and water as ballast could Binks maintain a reasonable trim. In all, seven fires broke out in the engine room. The food was so bad that Binks resorted to munching biscuits from the rations in the lifeboats.

Beneath a cheerless leaden sky, two salvage men proceed with the ignominious dismemberment of the Leviathan's hull as she lies grounded in the muddy shallows of Rosyth, Scotland. Only one of the four gigantic bronze-alloy screws on its inboard shafts remains intact, and the ragged V-shaped section of steel plate exposed above it is all that is left of the Leviathan's gracefully shaped stern.

One clear night in mid-Atlantic the wire triggering the steam whistle contracted from the cold, and a series of mournful blasts sounded over the waters, as if the *Leviathan* were grieving her own impending demise. After anchoring on the final night off Yaystack, a small Scottish island, the motley crew, demanding pay or else, went on strike. Binks's promises—and perhaps even more, the prospect of an indefinite stay on this inhospitable old derelict—persuaded them in the morning to take her in.

On Sunday, January 13, 1938, the *Leviathan* weighed anchor for the last time. When Binks turned the ship to sail under the Forth bridge, an oil pipe burst. The old monster proved no easier to steer to her slaughter than she had been to steer anywhere else. "She was a hoodoo ship all right," Captain Binks wrote with uneloquent bluntness to a friend after he was back safe in his cottage. "I was glad when we docked." As if to lay this giant ghost to rest once and for all, the No. 1 hold was flooded until the *Leviathan* sank in the mud at Rosyth. The breakers wanted to take no chances that the Scottish winter's high winds might blow Hull No. 212 about in a last skittish dance while they were cutting her up into small and unrecognizable pieces of metal.

O "Normandie"! O ship of light!

She was called the crowning triumph of the French Third Republic. She may not have been that, but she came close. Launched on October 29, 1932, the French Line's 80,000-ton *Normandie* was the biggest, swiftest and most sophisticated vessel afloat. She boasted the most advanced hull design, the most powerful engines, and her interior arrangements were awesome, not only for their size and complexity but for their ingenuity *(overleaf)*. Indeed, dining aboard the *Normandie* during her first visit to Southampton, Lord Runciman, a shipping magnate and Britain's foremost connoisseur of liners, remarked to one of his hosts: "You have an extraordinary ship here, but it is so advanced for its time that I ask myself if my countrymen will know enough to appreciate her as she deserves."

It might take an engineer to understand the *Normandie's* full technical triumph. But everyone could comprehend her magnificence. As no vessel before, and none after, she reached the outer bounds of luxury without ever falling over into mere extravagance. Only the French could combine the splendor of Versailles with the grace of a yacht. With accommodations limited to 1,972 passengers, the *Normandie* offered a spaciousness—at all levels—that was unprecedented on ocean liners. The 864 first-class passengers took their meals in the *grande salle à manger*, 60 feet longer than the Hall of Mirrors at Versailles; afterward they might repair to a theater that rivaled the houses of London or Broadway, or to a grand salon, aglitter with gold and crystal, for postprandial chatter.

For those seeking an informal atmosphere, the boat-deck grill, a restaurant-bar with walls done in varnished pigskin, ran a buffet all day and late into the night. Forward in the winter garden, a passenger could retreat among exotic caged birds, the spiked blades of tropical plants, fountains, aquariums and arabesqued marble arches hung with creepers. A gentleman feeling at a loss away from his club might find himself at ease again in the smoking room. There were swimming pools, libraries and boutiques, a shooting gallery, a kennel with its own sun deck, a hospital featuring an X-ray lab and operating theater and a lavishly ornate chapel on B deck that was transformed for Protestant services by a sliding panel that screened its Roman Catholic statuary.

The ordinary first-class staterooms, grander than those on other liners, came paneled in combinations of birch, oak, ash, mahogany, ebony, olive, cherry or walnut. No two were alike. And then there were 10 *suites de luxe*, one of which was a model of an actual chamber furnished in the Château de Bellevue, Paris, during the 18th Century for the Marquise de Pompadour. At the extreme of luxuriousness were the four apartments *de grand luxe* located on the upper and sun decks, each with four bedrooms, a sitting room (with a baby grand piano), dining room, pantry and four baths. Two of these suites were located on the sun deck and had their own promenades.

Accommodations for tourist passengers were as spacious as those for first-class on most other liners. The tourists dined, table d'hôte, in an ash-paneled salon crowned by an illuminated dome that reached three decks above their tables and was supported by five massive glass columns.

It cost $59 million to build the *Normandie*, and the French government footed most of the bill. Coming as it did in the bleakest days of the Depression, it seemed to some like a scandalous waste of funds. But for most Frenchmen, the *Normandie* was an act of faith in the future and a monument to France itself: beautiful, suave, possessed of great strengths but committed to style above all. "O *Normandie*! O ship of light!" declaimed a poet in a burst of emotional verse. A year after the *Normandie* made her maiden voyage, Britain's Cunard Line introduced its stately *Queen Mary*. But as an English lady once told the *Normandie's* captain, Pierre Thoreux: "In my opinion, the *Queen Mary* is a grand Englishwoman in sportswear—and the *Normandie* is a very gay French girl in evening dress."

Alive with the rustle of silk and the buzz of conversation, the Normandie's 300-foot grande salle à manger—the largest room afloat—fills with first-class passengers ready to dine. The captain's table, in this architect's rendering, is just in front of the large bronze statue representing peace. To either side, walls of hammered glass and cast-glass panels three decks high are illuminated from behind by lighting power equal to the brightness of 135,000 candles.

Tiles of enameled sandstone and bright mosaic wall friezes run the 75-foot length of the first-class swimming pool. Children kept to the terraced end (foreground), where they could practice between the stanchions set in the bottom. Beside the pool at the same end was a well-stocked bar and the doorway to the ship's gym.

Elegantly clad theatergoers arrive at the Normandie's 380-seat cinema/theater, the first to be installed on a liner. It was equipped with dressing rooms, wings and lighting gear, and often staged the latest hits from Paris, London and New York.

With its own Punch-and-Judy show and merry-go-round, the children's playroom in the deckhouse of the forward funnel kept youngsters as well entertained on the voyage as their parents were. The tykes also had their own dining room.

In the cavernous first-class smoking room, amid clusters of morocco leather settees and easy chairs, passengers could smoke and chat or read the *Normandie's* own daily newspaper from the ship's print shop. The walls are decorated with lacquered gold bas-reliefs depicting Egyptian sporting scenes. The great staircase to the rear leads to the grillroom, which served a buffet almost as elaborate as the regular menu.

Lighted by glowing fountains of crystal
and windows 22 feet high, the grand salon
was the very inner circle of the
Normandie's social life. Here passengers
took refreshment and danced in the
late afternoon, returning after dinner for
a concert or perhaps a gala ball.
The surrounding murals, etched in glass,
celebrated the history of navigation.

A glimpse into the sitting room of one of the four grand luxe apartments confirms the exceptional spaciousness of these Normandie accommodations. Inset above is a master bedroom.

The breezy vista from the Normandie's upper sun deck reveals an intricate pattern of territorial imperatives. The private promenade deck is at lower right. Below it, the first-class terrace is separated from the tourist-class promenade by a wood-and-glass partition, and beneath the tricolor at the stern is the third-class deck.

Chapter 3

The French Line: France's monument to itself

On the afternoon of May 29, 1927, Captain Joseph Blancart was sitting at a desk in his spanking new cabin on the *Ile de France*. It was 1:30, and Captain Blancart was anxiously cleaning up the preliminary reports that had to be completed before his ship put out to sea for her first trial run. In half an hour, high tide would crest and the *Ile de France* would leave the basin in Saint-Nazaire, cautiously nudged through the narrows by tugboats. Then she would pass through locks and be on her way to Le Havre. It was a moment that had been planned for weeks, for months—indeed, for years. Transat—as the Compagnie Générale Transatlantique, or the French Line, was known—had already built its share of distinguished transatlantic liners. None of them had won the Blue Riband, the trophy that signified the fastest ship afloat. But the *Ile de France,* which could make a moderate 24 or 25 knots, sought a subtler honor than speed: the distinction of providing ocean travelers with unexcelled luxuries of supreme comfort, of haute cuisine and impeccable service. When she floated out of Saint-Nazaire basin, leaving behind the Chantier de Penhoët shipyard where she had been 33 months in the building, the *Ile de France*, it was hoped, would quickly be recognized as the No. 1 great liner on the Atlantic.

All morning a French Navy band had been blaring from the quay for the benefit of the thousands of people who had gathered to be in on this moment of French history. Transat's handsome, aristocratic President John Henri Dal Piaz had been personally giving the grand tour of the ship to a party of government and industry dignitaries. Several hundred shipyard workers were still on board frantically finishing last-minute jobs. Just as frantically, the crew was preparing the vessel to sail.

In the midst of this sublime confusion the shipyard director and President Dal Piaz appeared in the doorway to tell Captain Blancart that the sailing would have to be postponed. Three more days were needed to finish installing faucets and light fixtures.

Blancart exploded on hearing the news. If the ship was to be kept at Saint-Nazaire for three days, he thundered, she would have to remain for 30 days. There would not be another tide high enough to float her 32-foot draft out of the shallow building basin for a month. Moreover, he knew she was ready. For the past two months he had been living aboard his ship, consulting with the marine architects who designed her and the engineers who built her. He knew her as well as a captain could know a ship before he had sailed her. He was determined not to delay any longer for such nonessential equipment as faucets and light fixtures, which could be installed during the trials.

Blancart won the argument. Dal Piaz had been prepared to consider a

Snug beneath soft plaid blankets, first-class passengers on board the French Line's famed Ile de France in 1931 take the bracing sea air as attentive stewards hover over them and proffer midmorning bouillon. The French Line rarely operated the fastest liners, but knew no equal when it came to luxury and service.

three-day postponement, but a month would endanger the schedule for the maiden voyage, already announced. And so at 1:30 p.m., when the captain was in his cabin with his paper work and the engines were warming up, the shipyard director was rushing about topside, arranging to have workers stay on board to do the finishing touches.

But at this point there occurred a fiasco. Exactly who was to blame, or why, has never been explained. Somehow, somewhere, someone heard, or thought he heard, an order to cast off and engage the engines, and the incredible deed was prematurely carried out. The nearly speechless shipyard director burst into the captain's cabin with the terrible message: *We're moving!*

Blancart rushed to the bridge. The impossible was happening. Not only was the *Ile de France* floating about unmoored; under influence of the engine's forward motion she was moving, and fast—in the direction of disaster. A huge shipyard crane hung over the basin. The *Ile de France* was drifting toward it. In a matter of seconds her mizzenmast would catch itself on the crane's boom and snap off. Desperately, Blancart put the helm hard over. The mizzenmast brushed by, undamaged. Then Blancart signaled the engine room: "Reverse engines, full speed astern."

Now a second calamity occurred. The engine room could not engage reverse. The engine controls had somehow jammed. Captain Blancart frantically scanned the tiny basin—this veritable bathtub in which he was forced to maneuver. The far end of the basin was boxed in by a drawbridge, and the runaway *Ile de France* was gaining momentum every minute. Blancart could see no way out. Tears were rising to his eyes, he later recalled, as he decided that his only option was to beach his lovely new ship. Blancart's hand was on the helm to drive her against the pier when, to his astonishment, he saw the drawbridge almost imperceptibly begin to rise. At first he thought he was hallucinating. He was not; the port lieutenant, seeing what was happening almost as quickly as Blancart himself, had raced to the controls of the drawbridge in order to give the *Ile de France* a second option.

It was not a very promising option. The drawbridge clearance, Blancart knew, was less than four feet on either side. Instead of being guided through slowly and gently by tugboats, he was bearing down upon this minuscule aperture in his 43,450-ton giant at a speed of more than 10 knots. Nevertheless, Captain Blancart decided to take the option. In doing so, he executed the most distinguished feat of seamanship of his distinguished career. Steady of hand, Blancart aimed the *Ile de France* at the passage—and skillfully whisked the 92-foot-beam ship through the less than 100-foot opening.

Just as the *Ile de France* sped toward the canal lock that stood between the bridge and the open sea, the engine room freed the controls. Blancart threw his 64,000-horsepower engines into reverse and dropped two anchors, halting the ship just before she went crashing into the unflooded canal lock. The first crisis of the *Ile de France* was past.

There had been an awful carelessness to the way the near-disaster began. But there had been such aplomb in the way the emergency was handled that the Gallic cry of "Vive Capitaine Blancart! Vive l'*Ile de France!*" had never been better deserved.

Bemedaled Captain Joseph Blancart of the Ile de France seems severe and humorless, but in fact he was gallant to ladies, beloved by his crewmen and tolerant even of stowaways. When perennial imposter "Prince" Mike Romanoff was caught stowing away aboard the France, he was treated to dinner before his arrest. He called Blancart "my favorite skipper."

This sort of flair, this panache on a tightrope, as it were, marked the French Line as a thing apart, even in an age when great liners abounded. As with certain other French achievements, the French Line ship was a compound of dash, grace, majesty and style, and a crossing on one was an irresistible blend of meticulous care and reckless spontaneity.

Exactly what made it so is hard to say. A much-traveled sophisticate of the '20s with the wonderful name of Basil Woon once took a stab at explaining it in a book about transatlantic voyaging. "English lines perhaps have a more distinguishable air of disciplined smartness," he wrote. "German cabin service is proverbial; 'efficiency' is a word which fits United States Lines boats; Italian lines err rather on the side of too much servility, which pleases most passengers; a speck of dirt on a Hollander ship might cause the Chief Steward to commit suicide." But a French Line ship? "There is an atmosphere about a French Line ship which is so subtle that you are unaware of its existence until the journey's end. You know that you have had a wonderful trip and a marvelous time. But you can't put your finger on any single incident or attention which is responsible."

Whatever the explanation, many an ocean traveler in the heyday of the great liners came to the conclusion that none surpassed the French Line in charm, finesse, elegance or luxury. The engineers and designers who built the ships, the crew and officers who staffed them—and even the passengers who had nothing to do but find ways to amuse themselves—all had a hand in creating the sublime concoction that was a French Line voyage in the 1920s and 1930s.

The very origins of the Compagnie Générale Transatlantique had involved a national gesture that was as flamboyant as any event in the later history of the company.

The French Navy had languished ever since its humiliating trouncing by the British under Lord Nelson at the Battle of Trafalgar in 1805. Just how low France had sunk became evident in 1854, when the nation entered the Crimean War to arrest Russia's expansion into European affairs: to transport her 30,000 troops to the battle scene, France had to charter ships from Britain, now her political bedfellow. The French merchant marine was no better off than the Navy. There were only a few passenger ships, and no service at all to the increasingly important North American ports; for such business as she conducted with the United States, France depended on foreign lines.

The Emperor, Napoleon III, riding a crest of nationalism after the successful conclusion of the Crimean War, was determined to assert French preeminence on the seas. He commissioned the first ironclad warships for the Navy. And to rebuild the merchant marine, he established Transat with a hefty government subsidy. It was to be a mail and passenger service that would send France's own ships to the United States, to the West Indies and to Mexico. More than any other of the great Atlantic carriers, Transat was to be both a corporation and a symbol of national pride. "In a confined space we produce our country," a French Line official once proudly stated, and certainly no other country put more of her personality into the ocean liner.

When the new firm was founded, two brothers, Emile and Isaac

Péreire, were appointed to head it. Between them they seemed to per-
sonify the qualities that would characterize the French Line. Emile,
with his deceptive angel face and bright eyes, was, in fact, shrewd and
ambitious; he was the realist in the family. Isaac—round, jolly, Parisian-
worldly in his air—was the idealist in the family. Together they made a
good team. Like many of the early great-liner entrepreneurs, the brothers
Péreire had been railroad pioneers, as well as successful bankers. They
came to their new undertaking, then, with obligatory patriotism, a prudent sense of the value of a franc and a slightly romantic notion of
seafaring, which was shared by their countrymen.

For its first ship, Transat turned to the steam-engine capital of the
world—Greenock, Scotland—and bought a large paddle-wheeler, to
which the brothers Péreire gave an American name, the *Washington,* in
honor of the nation that was to be the vessel's western destination. On
June 15, 1864, the 3,200-ton, 343-foot *Washington* began her maiden
voyage from Le Havre to New York, carrying some cargo, mail and 211
passengers, and the French Line was in business. Later that year the
Washington's sister ship, the *Lafayette,* emerged from the same yard in
Greenock, and in 1866 Transat purchased two screw-propelled vessels,
the *Péreire* and *Ville de Paris,* from the builder who started the Cunard
fleet: Napier's on the Clyde.

But nationalistic pride dictated that French ships be built by Frenchmen. Moreover, relationships between entrepreneurs and shipbuilders,
at best, were always delicate, fraught with all the usual tensions between
patrons and artisans. Transat devised a novel solution: the brothers
Péreire established their own shipyard. They bought some land near
the mouth of the Loire, and engaged a Scottish builder named John
Scott as a consultant. They called their new yard Chantier de Penhoët at
Saint-Nazaire, a felicitous name that was to evoke warbling praise from
great-liner connoisseur Ludwig Bemelmans. "*Chantier* is a lovely name
for a shipyard," he wrote. "It sounds like a song, like the name of a
beautiful songbird."

Modestly but steadily, Transat grew from 27 ships of all kinds—
freighters as well as passenger vessels—in 1865 to 69 in 1889. By then
Transat statisticians could boast that their fleet had made more than
1,632 voyages, covering more than 2,355,500 nautical miles. And
though the company never quite exceeded the mileage or the revenues of
its competitors across the Channel, the Cunards, it kept up with the
times in some unexpected ways. Isaac Péreire's son Eugéne, who served
as president of Transat from 1877 to 1904, was responsible for a number
of innovations. In the 1870s he converted all the old paddle-wheel ships
to screw propulsion. In the same decade his ships were the first to intro-
duce refrigeration in their cargo holds, and electric lighting above—
bringing passengers the kind of scientific progress that made possible
those convenient little luxuries for which French Line ships would be
noted. Eugéne Péreire also introduced another fillip with his liner the
Touraine. Crossing the Atlantic from New York to Le Havre in 1891 in a
record six days, 21 hours, she then proceeded on to Constantinople, with
passenger stopovers in the Azores and several Mediterranean ports—an
embryonic Mediterranean cruise. In more spartan days passengers had

Flying French and U.S. flags, as well as the
ensign of the Compagnie Générale
Transatlantique, the Washington steams
out of Le Havre in 1864, inaugurating French
Line passenger service to New York.

crossed the ocean just to get to the other side, but traveling was becoming so agreeable that the day of voyaging for its own sake was at hand.

Despite these successes, and despite an annual government subsidy of 11 million francs, in numbers of passengers the French still ran a poor third to the English and the Germans at the turn of the century. In 1902 the French Line, with 24,579 passengers, ranked fifth behind Hamburg-American (34,068), North German Lloyd (32,770), the English White Star Line (29,833) and Cunard (26,786). Owing to a combination of geographical convenience and political circumstance, Transat's share of emigration, the vital steerage trade, was sharply limited. English ships ferried the Irish, German ships the Central Europeans. Italian emigrants patronized the French Line as well as their own flag vessels, but there were not enough to tip the balance. In the peak years of 1907 and 1908, when emigration to the States topped one million, the French Line's share was scarcely 10 per cent.

Two other factors worked against Transat. One was that Le Havre, the line's home port, had originally been a fishing village, and despite more

With smoke belching from its many buildings and three new hulls rising on the stocks, the French shipyard Chantier de Penhoët in 1886 displays France's fierce commitment to its new shipping industry. "A mighty and sophisticated workshop" is how founder Emile Péreire envisioned the facility on the banks of the Loire in 1861. After 1866 all the great French Line ships, including the Ile de France and the Normandie, were built at Penhoët.

or less constant dredging, there were limits to the size of ship the little
port could accommodate. The other was that the building techniques of
the Chantier de Penhoët yard were hardly suited to giving birth to large
ships in a day of ever-increasing giants. Unlike the Clyde shipyards or
the shipyards of Hamburg and Bremen, Penhoët had few heavy cranes,
and no overhead structures or elevators to aid the workers. Instead, it
spread out horizontally; six miles of railroad connected the various an-
nexes of the 62-acre yard, indicating a certain lack of concentration.

And so the French Line went its stylish, firmly idiosyncratic way into
the 20th Century, but without quite ever becoming "the last triumph of
the Third Republic" that one tricolor-waving booster called for. Then, in
1912 Transat launched a vessel it named the *France* (not to be confused
with the later *Ile de France)*, and with that splendid ship the great liner
of unmistakably Gallic flair made her debut.

It was not in size that the *France* made her mark. Though she boasted
twice the tonnage of any previous French ship, at 23,769 tons she was
still only little more than half the size of Cunard's *Mauretania*, and less
than half the size of the Hamburg-American Line's monumental *Imperator* and *Vaterland*. Neither did she win any palms for smooth sailing.
She had an unfortunate tendency to roll. With a Gallic shrug, French

sailors said that it took a little rolling to make a little speed: "Bon rouleur, bon marcheur." But the *France*, even her most fervent admirers agreed, carried matters to an extreme: on her maiden voyage in April 1912 she broke $2,000 worth of crockery and fine porcelain.

Yet the *France* brought the French Line into the 20th Century in other important respects. She was the first of her nation's ships to mount four screws, and the first to be powered by a turbine, engineered, of course, under license from Charles Parsons. She also represented a departure in appearance: unlike British four-stackers of the period, which emphasized their vertical lines, the *France* took on a certain Parisian sleekness by having a broad white horizontal band painted between the somber black of the bow and the bridge. Actually, she towered as high above the water as any other ship, but the horizontal line gave her the optical illusion of being as low-slung as a seal.

But it was the *France*'s interior that made the real splash. Here the designers outshone themselves. Where German liners struggled heroically to emulate Wagnerian castles, and English liners fell into the dark-wood-and-leather habits of a London club, the *France* conjured up visions of a magnificent château on the Loire. The "Château of the Atlantic," as, in fact, she came to be called, set new records for gilded paneling. "I doubt that any craft since Cleopatra's fabled barge knew such visual extravagance," gasped one British observer. A life-sized portrait of the "Sun King," Louis XIV, copied from an original by Hyacinthe Rigaud in the Louvre, imperiously gazed down the length of the main lounge (the *salon de conversation*) at another portrait showing his royal self returning from the hunt. Between the two were rows of such dazzling beauties as Princess de la Tour du Pin, Duchesse de Bourgogne, Mme. de Maintenon—17th Century courtesans suggesting all the intrigue of the court of Versailles.

The private quarters were almost as sumptuous. The *cabines de grand luxe* could accommodate as many as six members of one family, who could sleep in canopied beds (no common shipboard bunks for *grand luxe* passengers on this floating palace), dine in privacy in their own Empire-style dining room ("For lunch on the days when you don't feel sociable—for dinner when you wish to entertain a couple of friends," crooned a *France* folder) and play cards in a drawing room copied from the salon in a Touraine château. And scattered about were all those little Gallic touches. On her dressing table, Madame found a device that instructed her to turn its little button and—*voilà!*—she heated "the intricate implements for completing the coiffure." Could a woman eager to primp for dinner ask for anything more? Or anything more French?

To pass from one deck to another, the *France* boasted a means of transportation that in 1912 was still a novelty ashore. "The citizen of the floating town presses a button, a grille rolls back to reveal an elevator, and he is whisked to the desired floor," as a dazzled passenger put it. But who would choose an elevator when the French had carried afloat that grandest of French architectural fancies, the staircase *(pages 104-105)*? The three-deck staircase on the *France*—all sweep and grand descent—was modeled after the one at the Bibliothèque Nationale with its bronze-filigree banister.

J. P. Morgan's great shipping gamble

Great Fleets of the Seven Seas
International Mercantile Marine Co.

AMERICAN LINE
LEYLAND LINE
ATLANTIC TRANSPORT LINE

RED STAR LINE
WHITE STAR LINE
WHITE STAR-DOMINION LINE

IMM

106 STEAMERS   1,028,592 TONS

Types of International Mercantile Marine Company's Steamers

Name	Gross Registered Tonnage	Name	Gross Registered Tonnage	Name	Gross Registered Tonnage	Name	Gross Registered Tonnage	Name	Gross Registered Tonnage	Name	Gross Registered Tonnage	Name	Gross Registered Tonnage	Name	Gross Registered Tonnage	Name	Gross Registered Tonnage
Adriatic	24,541	Belgian	5,287	Cufic	8,249	Karamea	5,624	Manchuria	13,639	Minnesota	20,602	Norseman	6,367	Rainga	10,940	Turcoman	5,828
Albanian	3,013	Bolivian	5,116	Demosthenes	11,223	Kroonland	12,241	Manhattan	8,112	Mississippi	4,736	Novian	6,368	Regina	16,313	Vedic	9,332
Alexandrian	4,467	Bovic	6,583	Dominion	7,257	Kumara	6,034	Maryland	4,711	Missouri	4,692	Nubian	6,384	Rimouski	9,280	Waimana	10,309
Antillian	5,624	Caledonian	4,998	Euripides	14,947	Lancastrian	5,134	Median	6,306	Mongolia	13,639	Olympic	46,439	Runic	12,489	Welshman	5,730
Arabic	18,000	Canada	9,415	Finland	12,223	Lapland	18,565	Medic	12,032	Montana	12,092	Oranian	1,942	St. Paul	10,230	Winifredian	10,428
Arawa	9,372	Canopic	12,097	Gallic	7,912	Mackinaw	3,204	Mesaba	8,002	Montreal	7,772	Orenza	7,996	Sanland	9,748	Zealandic	8,090
Asian	5,614	Cedric	21,039	Gothland	7,660	Mahana	11,796	Megantic	14,878	Napierian	6,410	Pakeha	7,911	Scythian	4,865	Zeeland	11,905
Athenic	12,345	Celtic	20,904	Haverford	11,635	Mahia	10,851	Merionian	6,306	Nessian	6,270	Persic	12,042	Suevic	12,531	TENDERS	
Baltic	23,876	Ceramic	18,481	Homeric	8,766	Mahopac	3,216	Minnetonka	6,919	Nevasan	6,569	Persian	12,042	Tainui	9,957	Nomadic	1,260
Barbadian	5,289	Corinthic	12,343	Indian	9,121	Maimoa	8,000	Mercian	6,305	New York	10,580	Philadelphia	10,233	Tauroa	8,000	Traffic	640
Bardic	8,010	Cornishman	5,749	Ionic	12,352	Maine	6,600	Michigan	8,162	Nisian	6,385	Philadelphian	6,585	Themistocles	11,231	Magnetic	619
Belgenland	24,547	Cretic	13,518	Irishman	9,530	Manuri	8,114	Minnekahda	17,221	Nitonian	6,381	Poland	6,649	Tropic	8,230	Total	1,028,592

Arrayed like a massive invasion fleet, the ships of J. P. Morgan's International Mercantile Marine Company appear to be smothering the ocean in this fanciful 1919 advertisement.

J. Pierpont Morgan is well remembered as a renowned banker, a canny railroad tycoon and the famed yachtsman who once advised: "The man who has to ask the price of a yacht cannot afford one." What is less commonly recalled is that he tried and failed to gain control of transatlantic shipping.

Morgan's raid on the sea-lanes began in 1900 when he was at the pinnacle of his power. His banking empire boasted assets of $162 million; his railroad combine included more than 29,000 miles from coast to coast; and his influence extended throughout United States industry. His shipping idea was simple: absorb the world's major shipping lines, then couple the ships with his rail networks to stretch, as an associate put it, "our railroad terminals across the Atlantic."

With a group of associates, Morgan & Company first put up $20 million to buy up America's two important shipping lines, the Atlantic Transport Company and the International Navigation Company. Thus Morgan acquired some 40 vessels, most of them freighters. He next focused on Britain. In April 1901 the syndicate laid out $12 million, in cash, for the more than 40 ships of the Leyland Line, the largest single transatlantic freighter operator. Ten months later, for $40 million in cash and stock, Morgan bought the White Star Line with eight liners, which at that time was turning a greater profit than Cunard's passenger service. Almost as an afterthought, Morgan snapped up Britain's Dominion Line with its handful of ships for a paltry $4.5 million.

At this point, after little more than a year, Morgan and his cohorts had acquired some 100 vessels, representing almost one fifth of all the tonnage then crossing between Europe and America, and a full third of the Atlantic passenger service.

In Europe the press railed against the "Morganization" of the Atlantic. But in shipping-line board rooms, businessmen found it hard to dismiss Morgan's proposals. Early in 1902 the two great German lines, Hamburg-American and North German Lloyd, quietly reached a 10-year agreement with Morgan's combine. While they would not sell out, they would affiliate with Morgan and agree on joint policies to avoid undue competition.

In April 1902 Morgan announced the formation of a parent holding company: The International Mercantile Marine Company, to be capitalized at $170 million. The figure was arrived at in part by calculating future stock values—which was optimistic indeed. In

"You may as well slide off into the water, old chap," says J. P. Morgan to Neptune in the text that accompanied this cartoon from 1902; "I'll boss the ocean from this on."

Britain the Cunard Line, with 17 liners and freighters, decided to fight a Morgan take-over. As London street vendors hawked "licenses to remain on earth," bearing the signature of J. Pierpont Morgan, Cunard's chairman pressured Parliament into a $11,712,000 loan to finance the building of new ships, plus an annual subsidy of $732,000.

Cunard's defiance heartened another major shipping line: France's Compagnie Générale Transatlantique, which operated 75 ships. The French Line turned a deaf ear to I.M.M., and now Morgan's grand design for transatlantic monopoly was in trouble. Matters grew even worse when the end of the Boer War in 1902 released scores of merchant ships for commercial service; freight rates plummeted, depressing the entire shipping world.

As Morgan's interest in the company declined, I.M.M. began to suffer from inept management; it entered receivership in 1915. However, the World War I demand for shipping saved the corporation from going under. It staggered on through the 1920s and '30s, selling off its foreign acquisitions and concentrating on its domestic holdings. The I.M.M. eventually changed its name to United States Lines Company and survived to profit as one of the biggest American shippers. But Morgan's dream of monopoly had long since died. "The ocean," said *The Wall Street Journal*, "was too big for the old man."

At the foot of the staircase the awed passenger found himself entering the main dining room with all the reverence owed to haute cuisine. Before each crossing 18 barrels of *pâté de foie gras* were shipped on board for canapés, and the rest of the menu took its standard from that, bringing to the *France* the exquisite cuisine that, from haut monde to peasant, is the ultimate expression of French well-being. From then on, a French Line passenger could routinely savor at a single meal a seven-course procession of such arcane delicacies as *potage Marie-Stuart, petites barquettes Sévigné, saumon de Loire à la Daumont, filet de Charolais à la Moscovite, faisans truffés* or *flanqués de cailles, asperges d'Argenteuil* and—before concluding with a sweet of *rochers de nougat*—wash down that surfeit of riches with Chambertin, that noble French Burgundy, at no extra charge.

Only two years after the *France* had put Transat firmly in the front ranks of transatlantic liners, World War I drove travelers off the ocean. For the first two years of the War, the *France* was laid up in a safely secluded anchorage. But then as the War progressed, she was brought out to serve, first as a hospital ship in the Mediterranean, and then as a troopship ferrying American doughboys across the Atlantic.

In 1918 the French Line emerged from the War, with the *France* unscathed and with big plans for the company. By 1920 the line also had a new man at the helm—the polylingually named John Henri Dal Piaz, grandson of an Italian anglophile and naturalized Frenchman. As a son of the Péreires' family doctor, John had been given a clerk's job in 1888. He repaid the favor well, working so hard he earned the position of chief secretary in nine years, and the presidency by the time the Péreires retired. "To live is not to copy; it is to create," Dal Piaz asserted. And with that credo he led the way in virtually creating the French Line anew for the high-living, high-spending 1920s. A year after he took over, the *France* was joined on the transatlantic run by the *Paris*—a 34,550-ton confection of shimmering Lalique glass and languid iron tracery—and in 1924 by the *De Grasse*, a ship that would be celebrated for her unfailing punctuality. Altogether the French Line had three great liners making regular crossings by the middle of the decade.

Like its competitor shipping companies, the French Line remodeled the old steerage quarters (which postwar immigration quotas had made obsolete), and turned them into something new called "tourist class"—not only upgrading accommodations, but heralding the arrival of a new social class as well: an ever-widening middle class that was emerging between the richest and the poorest of an earlier day.

Except for a brief recession in 1922, fortunes everywhere went up and up and up in the unprecedented economic boom of the postwar years. The French Line was not the least of those to profit. In 1919 the company lured 20,000 passengers aboard the *France*; as the fleet swelled, so did the number of passengers, rising to 75,000 in 1927 and to 91,000 in 1928—a four-and-a-half-fold increase in just a decade. In the same period, the company's income rose even more spectacularly—gross receipts more than doubled in a single year, mounting from 19 million francs in 1922 to 40 million in 1923. Thereafter they soared annually by leaps and bounds, reaching 189 million by 1928.

Though a hefty share of the French Line's rising fortunes came from the pockets of the newly prosperous middle class who sailed tourist, it was in first class that the line really scored. By 1929 Transat had won the lion's share of first-class passengers—and general acclaim for running the smartest ships afloat. All the promise held out by the *France* in 1912 thus came to flower in the 1920s.

On board the *France* or any other French liner, the crew and the officers were as much a part of the ambiance as the cuisine and the décor. Many of them became characters in their own right: the names of Henri Villar of the *Ile de France* and Roger Raulin of the *Paris*—French Line pursers who were known for their attentiveness—were chanted like a litany by knowledgeable travelers. Villar, for instance, kept files on regular passengers, complete with character sketches, and used the information to assemble congenial people when he made up dining table assignments. Crews included some outstanding amateur athletes, who competed in boxing, wrestling and fencing matches—providing entertainment for the passengers and engendering *esprit de corps* in the crew itself. French Line crewmen were "fiercely proud of their own ship," one French Line devotee wrote, "and sure she was the best of them all."

Among the exuberant men on these exuberant ships, none were more in evidence than the junior officers. Raoul de Beaudéan, a French Line officer who served for 34 years, rising from a junior officer to captain of the *Ile de France*, eventually wrote a nostalgic account of what it was like to be one such young officer aboard the *Flandre*, plying between Le Havre and the Americas during the 1920s.

The one word to describe their attitude was *esprit*. They had spirit and they had fun. Beaudéan told of one character among his compeers who rigged a radio to a hidden microphone. In the presence of passengers the radio would be "turned on." With appropriate cracklings and a slow rise in volume that sounded just like a shoreside 1920s radio, the hidden "announcer" would begin to deliver the news. As the listeners marveled at how clearly they were hearing Paris in the middle of the Atlantic, the jokester would lure them along with actual news bulletins on topical subjects. As Beaudéan recalled one incident: "With delight I hear a shrewish lady confide to her husband, 'You claim to be a radio specialist, but you couldn't get results like this at home!' " But then a report would issue from the speaker of a certain passenger's elderly uncle being arrested for committing an outrage against public decency and morality. Only at this point would the passengers realize that they were having their legs pulled, Gallic-style.

Sometimes the playful ruses extended into shipboard duties. The purser of the *Flandre* had a fake telephone installed in his office. By stepping on a button under his desk he could actuate a ring—the only function the phone was capable of. He would then pick up the receiver and with a voice full of awe say: "At your command, captain. Immediately." This was a discreet device for excusing himself from a boring passenger—a purser's occupational hazard even on the best of ships—without compromising his position as a French gentleman.

Such exuberant and youthful crewmen naturally found ways to enter-

In the Salon Mauresque on board the *France*, elaborate arabesque tiles combine with rich Oriental rugs, soft divans and plump leather ottomans to provide an exotic ambiance for her first-class passengers. With true Parisian hauteur, a French Line brochure promised that this Moorish hideaway would "seldom be found to harbor the tourist in need of a Baedeker or the presuming person of doubtful antecedents."

tain themselves off duty. One of the more artistic officers decorated the walls of the officers' dining hall with risqué cartoons; one, entitled "Night Patrol," was a sketch of the artist himself admiring a very barely clad young woman through a porthole.

The dining hall now resembled a Paris café, and the *Flandre* officers carried the idea further, detaching the dining table and chairs, originally fastened to the deck, so that the space could be cleared to make a dance floor. To this location the officers invited the belles of the passenger list, and danced the nights away.

When not on night watch, eligible young officers were expected by their captain to turn up in the main salon after dinner to be available as dancing partners for the ladies. "This courtesy, rare on transatlantic liners," Beaudéan pointed out, proved to "our captain the immensity of our devotion to the commonweal"; many a wallflower and many a dowager would have crossed the Atlantic danceless but for the gallantry of the young officers.

To assume that the officers of a French liner were mere *boulevardiers* would be a grave mistake. Witty and sophisticated hosts belowdecks, they were serious and competent seafarers on the bridge. Most had been thoroughly trained as Navy midshipmen or in the merchant marine before turning to liners. They learned everything from ship maintenance to pilotage and navigation. The result was a corps of expert navigators capable of such formidable feats as the one by which Captain Blancart saved the *Ile de France* in her moment of peril at Saint-Nazaire.

When she entered the fleet in 1927—joining the *France,* the *Paris* and the *De Grasse*—the *Ile de France* brought to four the number of great French liners plying the Atlantic Ocean. Of them all, the *Ile* was in some special fashion the most wonderful, the most chic, the most French, and soon she owned the hearts of her passengers. Her 43,450 tons did not come up to the *Vaterland,* by now renamed the *Leviathan.* And, of course, she never won the Blue Riband, in an age that prized speed above all. But no matter. She had a special verve; she was the jazz-age flapper of flappers. With her 29-foot bar—where Americans could flout Prohibition, drinking Scotch at 15 cents a glass—and her "sidewalk" café, the *Ile de France* signaled what a lot of the world wanted to hear after the War, and after the fatigue and doubt of the early '20s: "The old days are back. Let the good times roll!"

Like every Transat ship that had gone before her, the *Ile de France* was lavish in décor. With 40 columns soaring in her main lounge, she evoked an elegant Classicism; with her varnished wood veneer discreetly sheathing fireproof steel underpinnings, she was modern without being vulgar. A hefty share of the 1920s oceangoing public found that the *Ile* was an agreeably modish place to sit out an ocean crossing, a fact evident from the quarter of a million passengers who made 347 crossings on her in the next 12 years.

Like other Transat ships, the *Ile de France* had stellar personnel; Captain Blancart in particular proved himself as able a navigator in the lounge as on the flying bridge. One night in the 1920s when the great dancer Argentina was scheduled to perform, the ship was pitching and rolling so violently that Argentina thought she might have to cancel her show. But Captain Blancart was not the person to allow a little Atlantic tempest to interfere with art. According to the story later circulated, Blancart halted his vessel, opened her fuel vents and flooded the surrounding water with a film of oil, thus calming the turbulent sea and permitting Argentina to dance upon a deck as steady as though she were in port. Captain Blancart later vehemently denied the oil part of the story; all he had done was to alter the ship's course and head the bow into the wind for the duration of Argentina's performance.

The rival Cunard skipper Arthur Rostron once complained that every transatlantic liner had three sides: port, starboard and social. No such complaint would be likely to cross the lips of Captain Blancart, who was always ready with a gallant gesture. On one voyage during the '20s, a certain Mme. Mathis—beautiful, impulsive and the very rich wife of an automobile manufacturer—confided to the captain at his table that she simply adored listening to music while having her bath. The next day Madame had no sooner stepped into her tub than the ship's orchestra assembled outside her suite to serenade her for a soapy hour or so.

Such passengers contributed to the *Ile*'s cachet no less than her distinguished crew and officers. Among them they joined in making life aboard seem to be a floating party—sometimes by quixotic demands like

For size and complexity, the first-class kitchens on the France, shown here in a 1912 cutaway, rivaled those of the grand restaurants of Paris. Special features in French Line kitchens included rims surrounding the main cooking and serving surfaces so that not a drop of goodness would be lost if the vessel happened to roll. A staff of chefs and assistants concocted meals of such delectability that the line claimed overeating became a "sport and clients of the French Line always abused their digestions to perfection."

Dressed in immaculate white uniforms, their hats as high as perfect soufflés, 35 chefs of the France pose at the foot of the grand staircase leading into the dining room. "Just when you think the height of artistry has been reached," one French Line official crooned, "the smiling steward presents a different treat."

Mme. Mathis', sometimes by virtue of their celebrity, often by the panache with which they brought themselves onstage.

The latter was the case with Ernest Hemingway, still an unestablished author. As Hemingway told the story, he was traveling to Paris, cabin class. A friend with a spare tuxedo invited him to the first-class dining room. One evening a "spectacle in white" materialized at the top of the *Ile*'s magnificent staircase, then slowly descended as every eye in the room watched. It was Marlene Dietrich. When she went to join her table, she discovered that she would make an unlucky 13th and effected to leave. The gallant (or conniving) Hemingway, who was seated within earshot at another table, leaped to his feet, and solved the problem—by volunteering to make the party 14. Hemingway's act won the attention of the entire dining room.

Another passenger—"Prince" Mike Romanoff, the social lion and frequent stowaway—was even bolder. On one memorable occasion he slipped aboard the *Ile de France* by befriending no less a person than United States Secretary of the Treasury Andrew Mellon on the boat train. Romanoff then passed himself off as a part of the Mellon entourage. A few days later, when confronted on the grand staircase as a passenger who had no cabin—that is, as a stowaway—he proclaimed with a wave of his hand, "The entire ship is my cabin," and majestically descended to dinner. The *Ile de France* crew, appreciating a grand gesture when they saw one, served him dinner, after which they tactfully incarcerated him for the duration of the voyage.

The more daring the gesture, the better the *Ile* passengers liked it. One March morning in the early 1930s the *Ile de France* had just left the shores of France, en route to Plymouth to pick up more passengers on her westbound run, when a black speck appeared in the sky. Coming closer, it proved to be a little Blackburn Bluebird biplane. The pilot caught up with the ship, circled her, swooped low, waggled his wings and, at the low point of his dip, waved from the open cockpit.

On the deck below was a pretty young woman named Dorothy Paine, of a prominent New York family. During her stay in Paris Dorothy had been escorted about town by Pierre Van Laer, the charming son of a wealthy cotton broker. When it came time to say au revoir, Pierre told Dorothy she would see him again. Now he was keeping his promise: in the blustering wind he was the young man in the sky paying homage to his love below, as if in a Romeo and Juliet scene played upside down. After appropriate flourishes from above and wafted kisses from below, Van Laer circled one last time and headed home. Moments later the crowd that had assembled on deck watched in horror as the Bluebird's engine sputtered and the little plane went down.

In an instant, Captain Blancart ordered the ship halted; then he turned her around and retraced his wake at full speed for two or three miles. Cautiously he reduced to half speed. When the *Ile de France* arrived in the vicinity of the plane crash, there was no trace of wreckage, and no sign of Van Laer. The freezing, choppy waters made his chances of survival seem dim even if he had managed to stay afloat. Just as everyone had given up hope, Van Laer was spotted—almost as tiny a figure in the water as he had been in the sky. A lifeboat was lowered to fetch him, and

A "beau geste" of grand staircases

Of all the national characteristics of décor, none marked a French liner so indelibly as the grand staircases leading to her various salons and dining rooms. With sweeping architectural exuberance they descended tier upon tier, sometimes piercing three entire decks. Above them vaulted extravagant domes and illuminated ceilings; the balustrades were ribbons of stainless steel or arabesques of wrought iron leading down heavily carpeted marble steps. On the landings were dazzling vistas of mirrors, or towering oil paintings that were set off by gilded angels, polished brass fittings or intricately inlaid tiles.

To one observer, it was all slightly gauche, a calculated effort "to stun impressionable Americans with an overkill of grandeur." But the French Line took such sour comments in stride. "Low ceilings," as one brochure put it, "do not aid the appetite."

The French held the Renaissance view that life at its best is art, nowhere more sublimely staged than in the drama of making a grand entrance—the gentleman in white or black tie, the lady on his arm superbly coifed and gowned as they gracefully descended a magnificent staircase.

To ensure an appropriate setting, the French Line modeled its staircases after those in France's historic palaces and châteaux. With the decline of monumental architecture in the 20th Century, French ships became splendid and rare examples of this elegant marriage of function and form.

Modeled on the grand staircase in the 18th Century mansion of the Count of Toulouse, the entrance to the main dining room of the France is a gilt and marble exercise in Louis XIV opulence. In the painting, ladies at Versailles are helped by periwigged dandies to a swan boat in a pool on the palace grounds.

Fine filigrees of wrought iron—featuring a stork and a lion in a palm-fringed glade—mark the balustrades of the mirror-backed double staircase on the Paris. The ironwork and elaborate glass ceiling create the impression of a formal winter garden in a French château.

Swirling geometric patterns spilling from landing to landing in the grand salon of the Paris make the staircase a showpiece of Moorish décor. The arabesques of the illuminated dome, soaring arches, mosaic tiles and staircase are modeled on the palaces of French North Africa.

Breaking with tradition, the grand staircase of the Ile de France shies away from Versailles-period architecture in favor of Art Deco. Nonetheless, the combination of marble, calculated angles, mirrors and polished brass creates a spectacular descent through three tiers.

soon the very wet, very cold young man was brought on board—managing a grin and a wave to Dorothy.

Van Laer had no money with him, and no passport. Yet after a day in the ship's hospital, he suddenly appeared on the passenger list. He also appeared in the dining room, wearing Captain Blancart's spare dinner jacket. His mother had paid his round-trip passage by cable. Even had Mama not offered a sou, he most likely would have been welcomed aboard ship. Van Laer was just the kind of man to find the *Ile de France* congenial—and she him. He possessed the proper recklessness, the '20s style, and the luck of the ship herself.

Of all the great liners, the *Ile de France* may have come the closest to transforming a passenger list into a community. "The *Ile de France*," one of her appreciators wrote, "somehow inspired in her guests the will to live merrily, if only for the moment." Another went even further, suggesting that in her sophistication "the *Ile de France* was perhaps the floating incarnation of a consistent American fantasy about France and the French." When good Americans die, they go to Paris—or so Oscar Wilde claimed—and more than one American in the '20s and '30s would have suggested that the travelers might have arrived at their destination via the *Ile de France*.

Yet the *Ile de France*, like her captains and crews, was far more than a scintillating show of glamor and gesture. She was one of the most reliable great liners in history. She went to the rescue of other ships nine times in her career. She never suffered an accident of her own. Underneath all the playgirl décor, partying and general spirit of Montmartre-on-the-Atlantic was a working ship. On this point French Line seafarers never became confused. "Sir," said a Transat purser to a Transat captain, "you are the driver of a tramway of which I am the collector of fares."

If the *Ile de France* was the ship of the '20s, the ship of the '30s was the glorious *Normandie (pages 80-89)*. What a liner she was! A sour minority of Frenchmen derided her as France's "floating debt" when she was launched on October 29, 1932, in the depths of the Great Depression and at the astronomical cost of almost $60 million. However, most Frenchmen greeted the liner with paeons of praise. "What palace, what Triumphal Way, what memorial have we built to perpetuate our civilization, as the cathedrals perpetuate that of the Middle Ages, the castles of the Loire that of the Renaissance, and Versailles that of the age of Louis XIV?" cried one overwrought patriot. What else but the *Normandie*? Another Frenchman summed her up more succinctly as "unrealistic, impractical, uneconomical and magnificent." Many Englishmen and Americans agreed that the *Normandie* represented not only the culmination of all the beauty, grace, style and finesse that Transat, now just four years short of its 75th anniversary, had been evolving, but the *pièce de résistance* of all the great liners.

The *Normandie* became a symbol of national mystique. The playwright Jean Giraudoux wrote that not only was the *Normandie* the end product of the extraordinary strength and skills of the superior men who built her, plus the superior materials they built her with, but she was also the floating embodiment of the will and the soul of France. French

President Albert Lebrun noted, "Often in the past the World has said that Frenchmen created on too small a scale. This time no such reproach can be addressed to us, and let us have the courage of our great audacity. Forward with *Normandie!*"

When the *Normandie* was launched on that late October day, she slid down the greased ways at a speed approaching 17 knots and pulled a hundred or so madly scrambling spectators into the water in her backwash. The launching provided an appropriately sensational commencement for a ship that was meant to sweep all before her—a ship that could do nothing undramatic.

As the chapel, with its nave two decks high, was consecrated, it seemed necessary for a member of Transat to assure the officiating cardinal: "Eminence, those who built this fast and luxurious liner have not committed the sin of pride. They desired that, in international competition, France should be represented by an entry worthy of her." Given the

As officers on the bridge of a nearby vessel doff their caps in salute, the 792-foot Ile de France steams through the Atlantic after her maiden voyage in June 1927. Though neither the largest nor the fastest of liners, the ship was very popular. "She was handsome," said one chronicler, "without being grand, comfortable without being overstuffed, class-conscious without living by exclusions."

larger explanation—and the imminent presence of the *Queen Mary*, about to be launched across the Channel—the cardinal agreed.

Of the nearly 100 vessels that now made up Transat with a total gross tonnage of nearly 700,000—including its freighters and vessels sailing the Mediterranean and Oriental routes—the *Normandie* was the largest by far. At a length of 1,029 feet, she had 10 feet on the Cunarder *Queen Mary*; and at her ultimate 83,000 tons, she was 2,000 tons greater than the *Queen Mary*. But these were mere materialistic drum rolls. The *Normandie*'s true triumph was in her design. She was unique, from her rakish clipper bow to the magnificently rounded overhanging counter on her stern. Her hull was the concept of a Russian emigré named Vladimir Yourkevitch, who had designed warships for the Czar before the 1917 Revolution. The clean-swept look of her superstructure was a contrast to the cake-topping fussiness characteristic of other great liners, and evoked comparisons with thoroughbred horses and birds of the air. When she was put through her paces off Britanny, the local sardine fishermen lined up to watch, and these most skeptical of critics were impressed by the astonishing absence of the heavy waves that usually issued from a great liner's wake. Instead of plowing through the Atlantic, the fishermen reported, the *Normandie* glided over the water like a gull—though she was averaging more than 31 knots. Indeed, the sleek lines of the hull gave her amazingly little wake for so large a ship.

Her construction and equipment, like her design, were ahead of the times. Fire was always a major concern in shipbuilding. The Chantier de Penhoët shipyard was determined that the *Normandie* "should approach as nearly as possible to a 100 per cent fireproof ship." Toward that end they fireproofed all bulkheads, building some of aluminum, others of composite metal and wood with asbestos insulation, and they installed doors that were to close electrically from a central control switch in case a fire should start.

As if the *Normandie*, with her cast-glass paneling and hidden lighting was not avant-garde enough, she carried among the equipment on her bridge a brand-new device that had been invented by Maurice Ponte, a Parisian engineer. It was an instrument for detecting ships and icebergs up to four miles distant by means of radio waves that swept the horizon port and starboard in 45° arcs. When the beam encountered an obstacle, it rebounded to a receiver, and an amplified beep could be heard in a telephone on the bridge. Therefore the *Normandie* could lay claim to carrying the first rudimentary radar.

Her maiden voyage was nothing less than a triumph—prepared for and executed with a flourish that only the French Line's nonpareil hosts could muster. Not surprisingly, cuisine had high priority in the planning; thousands of bottles of wine were shipped on board months in advance, to allow their contents to settle properly. Freight cars came right to the side of the hull to deliver tons of fresh fruits and vegetables from Paris. With typical French Line forethought—and perhaps a small shudder—the galleys were also stocked with such American delights to the palate as ketchup, hominy grits, cranberry sauce and malted-milk powder. Entertainment ran a close second to food; the Paris Opera's *corps de ballet* arrived in Le Havre in a chartered train for a special

MENU
DU
Mercredi 13 Octobre 1937

Menu Suggestion

Hors-d'Œuvre à la Française

Coquilles Saint-Jacques
à la Mode de Saint-Malo

Salsifis aux Fines Herbes

Contrefilet Grillé Maison
Pommes en Liard

Salade de Saison

Le Plateau des Fromages

Pâtisserie Parisienne

Glaces Variées

Corbeille de Fruits

PAQUEBOT

" NORMANDIE "

A veritable cornucopia of gustatory delights graces the Normandie's luncheon menu cover, painted by a noted French artist of the day. But the still life is as nothing compared to the Lucullan feast presented within. A diner ordering à la carte (below) could choose among nearly 30 hot or cold offerings, while the menu suggestions (below, left) promised a nine-course triumph of haute cuisine. In both cases, the hors d'oeuvre cart deserves special mention; a determined gourmand could sample 13 items ranging from green olives to rabbit terrine.

LUNCHEON

Green Olives · Celery · Black Olives
Stuffed Onions Ménagère · Tourangelle Salad
Rolled Smoked Salmon · Stuffed Eggs Mustard Sauce
Paris Sausage · Lentil Salad
Rollmops and Bismarck Herrings
Canapés Epicurienne · Marinette Salad
Terrine of Young Rabbit St-Hubert

Hot Consommé · Chicken Consommé
Onion Soup · Italian Paste Consommé
Potage Fermière

Hungarian Omelet
Poached Eggs Bénédict
Scrambled Eggs with Ham
Cold Eggs Wladimir

Dabs Grenobloise
Saint-Jacques Shells à la Mode de Saint-Malo

LA ROGNONNADE DE VEAU MIJOTEE A LA LYONNAISE

Stewed Lamb and New Vegetables
Gnocchi à la Romaine

Buttered New Lima Beans
Carrots in Butter
Salsifys with Sweet Herbs

Mashed · Baked · A l'Anglaise · Jacket
Liard Potatoes

Spaghetti · Noodles · Macaroni (Baked 10 minutes)
Rice · Rice with Curry

Broiled Fillet of Beef Maison
Broiled Mutton Chops à l'Anglaise
Loin of Pork Apple Sauce

Virginia Ham · Bayonna Ham · York Ham
Ham « des Ardennes » · Prager Ham
Beef Mode in Jelly · Loin of Veal in Jelly Printanière
Cold Rack of Pork · Cold Chicken
Cold Rib of Beef · Foie Gras à la Gelée au Porto
Saddle of Lamb
Cold Turkey Red Currant Jelly
Lobster Mayonnaise · Fillets of Sole Monégasque

Mache · Chicory · Riviera Salad · Mixed
Potato Salad · Mexican Salad

Neufchâtel · Reblochon · Port-Salut
Brie · Chester · Provoloni

Florentine Cream · Fruit Pudding · Peach Pie

Assorted French Pastry

Vanilla · Plombières · Chartreuse · Tangerine

Assorted Fruits
Stewed Fresh Fruits

Bordeaux Rouge Supérieur · Bordeaux Blanc Supérieur
Bourgogne Blanc Supérieur

China Tea · Ceylon Tea · Orange Pekoe
Vervain · Linden Tea · Mint · Camomille
American Coffee · French Coffee · Sanka Coffee

performance in the grand salon on the *Normandie's* last evening in port. And to provide entertainment for the crossing, the first passengers, permitted to board a day early, were actors scheduled to open the *Normandie's* theater at sea with the first performance of a new comedy by François de Croisett. Commanding the ship was Captain René Pugnet, who had succeeded Blancart in command of the *Ile de France*; the purser was the famed Henri Villar, also from the *Ile de France*. The ratio of crew to passengers was more than one to one: 1,300 crew, 1,013 passengers. Among the latter were Mme. Albert Lebrun, wife of the President of France; Pierre Cartier, the Paris and Fifth Avenue jeweler; Mrs. Frank Gould, wife of the financier; dress designer Jean Lanvin, and the Maharaja of Karpurthala.

Gliding across the Atlantic at 30 knots, the *Normandie* entered New York Harbor on June 3, 1935, to a tumultuous welcome. The "Marseillaise" blared from the loudspeaker of an airplane circling overhead. Along the banks of the Hudson, 30,000 spectators watched from the Manhattan side, and another 100,000 from the New Jersey side. On the river itself, a multitude of small craft raced to keep up with the *Normandie* as she gracefully eased up the Hudson; a flotilla of fireboats shot plumes of white water up into the air; and a tugboat towed a helium-inflated Mickey Mouse.

On board, the celebration was as joyous as on the river. The crossing had been made in a record four days, three hours and 14 minutes—earning the French Line the coveted Blue Riband, for the past 10 years held by the Italian liner *Rex*. Sharing the triumph with the passengers, the French Line produced from the purser's safe 1,300 commemorative medals, each with the ship's name and the date, and each with a miniature blue ribbon. And, announcing the triumph from the masthead, she hoisted a 30-meter blue pennant—a meter for every glorious knot. Captain Francesco Tarabotto of the *Rex* cabled congratulations to Captain Pugnet, saying his ship was giving up the Blue Riband "with a smile."

In 1936, on its 75th anniversary, the Compagnie Générale Transatlantique seemed at last to rule the Atlantic. Five Transat liners were making crossings from Le Havre to New York: the *Paris*, the *Ile de France*, the *Lafayette*, the *Champlain* and the *Normandie*, which was the *femme magnifique* of them all. Each liner was spankingly modern; only the *Paris* was more than 10 years old.

But the wave of Transat had crested. Horror and disaster loomed. On May 5, 1938, the *Lafayette* burned at her dock in Le Havre, of causes unknown, and the hull was sold to shipwreckers. Less than a year later the *Paris* suffered a fire in the same place; this time French Line officials suspected arson by saboteurs. But they were unable to prove it. And catastrophe lay in wait for even the beautiful and unparalleled *Normandie*.

In 1939, after four years of service, the *Normandie* had logged 139 crossings and carried 133,170 passengers. There was no reason to suspect that she would not undertake many more swift and luxurious passages. However, when she departed from Le Havre on August 23, 1939, she embarked on what was to be her final journey. She docked in New York Harbor on August 28; four days later Germany marched into Poland, France joined England in declaring war, and World War II descended like a poisonous fog on civilization.

Transatlantic travel was finished for civilians for the duration, and for safekeeping, the French government left the beautiful ship in the United States. For the next two years the *Normandie* lay on the south side of Pier 88 in the Hudson River, guarded from Nazi sabotage by the United States Coast Guard. In June of 1940 France fell under Nazi occupation. Then came Pearl Harbor on December 7, 1941, and five days after that the United States—not only in the War now but committed to supply troops by the hundreds of thousands—seized the *Normandie* and began preparations for converting her into a troopship: painting her smart black-and-white hull a dull war gray, and removing from her interior such tokens of her former splendor as 18,000 bottles of wine, six pianos and four hobbyhorses, which were sold to the public several months later. Meanwhile, she had orders to sail for Boston on February 14, 1942.

As the date drew near, a force of 800 civilian workmen, 300 Naval personnel and 400 Coast Guardsmen, goaded by wartime urgency, worked at a hectic pace to get the *Normandie* ready. To accommodate the 14,000 troops that were expected to be crowding into her, the vast grand salon was made even larger by the removal of the partition that had separated it from the smoking room. Thousands of feet of carpeting were rolled up and stashed in passageways alongside rolls of linoleum that would be laid in its place. Throughout the vessel, doors came down and telephone wires were disconnected. And for everything old that was taken out, something new was brought in. In this lot were 14,130 new kapok life preservers that arrived from a Brooklyn factory, wrapped by the bale in tarred paper and burlap; they were dumped helter-skelter, most of them in the enlarged grand salon, which was the most convenient place for storing the life preservers until they could be distributed to the cabins below.

The morning of February 9 dawned bright and cold, with a stiff wind blowing across from the west bank of the river. Of the hundreds of jobs scheduled for the day, one was to cut off the four deck-to-deck stanchions that had provided illumination for the grand salon in palmier days. Three of the stanchions came down without incident. About 2:30 p.m. Clement Derrick, an employee of the Robins Dry Dock and Repair Company, was ready to tackle the fourth. "Down with the old apple tree!" called an irreverent naval inspector who was passing by. Somebody noticed that several bales of life preservers were lying right there at the foot of the stanchion. The order was given to move them, and they were moved—about two feet.

Derrick raised his arm and flipped a switch, and blue-white flame shot from the nozzle of his torch. Sparks flew. And the kapok life preservers, those highly flammable instruments of survival, burst into flames. There was not a fire extinguisher in the room, and not a single trained fireman in sight. The nearest hose was on the promenade deck. In an instant the flames had leaped from bale to bale, crossed to the port wall of the salon, swept down the length of the room and out its doorless end. In another instant, smoke was pouring down the ventilation ducts and elevator shafts. When it reached the engine room, the startled crew swiftly shut down the generators—and the ship's power. The lights went out; the remaining automatic fire doors that the French builders had installed were rendered inoperative; and water pressure sank to zero, so that when someone reached the hose on the promenade deck, all he could get from it was half a bucket of water.

At that point the fire was already spreading so quickly that the only thing on the minds of most of those present was escape. In a matter of minutes, hundreds of workmen were crowding into the darkened corridors and groping their way along unfamiliar passageways. Reaching the deck, one group seized a lifeboat and lowered it into the ice-choked Hudson River and rowed themselves to safety. Two other workmen dived from the bow and were rescued, half-frozen, by the fireboats that were now gathering around the stricken *Normandie*. Hundreds more workmen rushed to the gangplanks—where, compounding the already irremediable catastrophe, they caused massive congestion, colliding with New York City firemen who were clambering up with hoses, ladders and axes in hand.

Incredibly, the fire had been raging for 11 minutes before the alarm reached the New York City fire station at 12th Avenue and 49th Street, only about a block away. However, as soon as the word was out, every available piece of equipment on the city's West Side responded to the alarm; 43 fire engines clanged through the streets; Mayor Fiorello H. LaGuardia raced uptown from city hall and installed an impromptu office on the pier; and 30,000 spectators surged into the neighborhood. Two companies of the United States Army had to be summoned to drive the crowd back as far as 11th Avenue.

It took only half an hour for the fast-spreading fire to ravage the ship. Nonetheless, the city's fire-fighting forces did what they could, working frantically under the glare of emergency floodlights that were brought to the site as night came on. By 8:30 p.m. LaGuardia was able to announce that the fire was out. The problem now was to maintain the *Normandie*'s upright position; an estimated 100,000 tons of water had been poured into her blazing port side, and she was beginning to list. Tugboats were already pushing against the port side to keep her from capsizing—to no avail. By 10 o'clock she was listing 16°. As the tide rose, the list grew worse, and at about 12:20 a.m. the order was given for all hands to abandon ship. The tugs moved away as well. At 2:35 a.m., almost exactly 12 hours after Clement Derrick had fired his acetylene torch, the *Normandie* turned slowly over to port until she rested on her side in the mud of the Hudson.

Strangely, in spite of the presence of so many thousands of people in all that inferno, the casualties were small in number: 128 injuries and one fatality. The latter was Frank Trentacosta, a workman who fell to the pier when attempting to flee from the ship, and died in a hospital about 7 o'clock that evening.

But the *Normandie* herself was a casualty of the first magnitude. She made a cruelly surreal and nightmarish sight. Two of her propellers were in view and her funnels were only inches above the ice-caked surface of the water. During the next two days, the *Normandie* slowly settled at the stern in 42 feet of frigid water. To a *Normandie*-lover, the sight, which was all too visible to motorists along the West Side Highway, was unbearable—a travesty of everything that the ship had been. Ludwig Bemelmans wrote: "Every time I pass, along the West Side Highway, a spot just above 46th Street, there comes over me the feeling that I experience at the dentist's as I wait for him to get through putting the little drill in his machine."

Because of the War, the question of sabotage naturally arose, a specter that inquiries by House, Senate, Naval and city judicial committees put to rest. New York District Attorney Frank S. Hogan summed up the findings succinctly: "There is no evidence of sabotage," he declared. "Carelessness has served the enemy with equal effectiveness."

Every effort was made to salvage the beautiful ship. Vladimir Yourkevitch, the designer of the *Normandie*'s hull, who had left France to settle in the United States in 1939, thought she could be raised in four or five months if a series of dams were constructed within the semisubmerged ship, and then pumped out one by one.

A year later the operation to right the *Normandie* was still going on, and no progress was in sight. But eventually the pumping worked. In August 1943 the *Normandie* began her rise from the mud. By October 27—after 18 months of work and $19,200,000 in expenses—the *Normandie* floated upright in her dock. Twenty tugs towed the stained and scarred hulk down the Hudson River and around to Brooklyn. Just a few days after D-Day, when Allied troops were landing in France, the Navy gave up all thought of rebuilding France's greatest ship. On September 20, 1945, the *Normandie* was declared to be "surplus property." The French government was awarded $13 million in damages, and what remained of the ship was put up for bid. The winning bidder was one Julius Lipsett of 80 Wall Street, who offered $161,680 and then proceeded to cut up the *Normandie* for scrap.

When the *Normandie* was launched, she was given a motto, *Fluctuat nec mergitur*, which translated "She may be tossed but not submerged." Alas, her bold motto failed her. Yet in a poetic sense, the spirit of the *Normandie* was never submerged. More than two decades later, when the French Line launched another flagship, a ship-loving poet expressed just how much afloat the *Normandie* remained in the collective memory of her adoring fans:

The Channel clouds; the ships merge utterly;
Our faith now is in the France, for good or ill.
But when the bored foresake the guarding rail,
The life preserver, spotlit, still reads Normandie.

Gutted by fire, the Normandie lies on her side in the mud of a Hudson River berth as a fireboat pours water into her smouldering hull. "It requires an effort of the imagination," wrote The New York Times, "to realize that that great hulk of a once proud ship lying on her beam is not suffering humiliation. The sight of her hurts the human eye and heart."

Chapter 4

A litany of disasters on the devil sea

n every ship venturing forth on the North Atlantic there is a special load-line mark painted on the hull. It is the lowest and most cautious of all load lines, and it is identified as "WNA"—Winter North Atlantic. This is the line beyond which a vessel must never be loaded in that season on that ocean. No other ocean has ever inspired any such mark of fear and respect.

Absolutes of violence are difficult to define, and still more difficult to prove. The misnamed Pacific, with its shrieking typhoons, can on occasion produce greater waves and higher winds; the Indian Ocean, with its implacable monsoons, can play host to more sustained storms; the southern seas around Africa and South America can be terrible to contemplate. But for sheer unremitting menace, with every horror that is known to the sea, including fog, ice and the interacting furies of wind, wave and current, the North Atlantic has earned its reputation as the most dangerous body of water in the world. It is also the ocean on which man has chosen most often to sail; for that reason its perils loom more significant still.

"The natural hazards to be met on this ocean defy invention and read like a seasonal catalogue from hell," one chronicler has written with a kind of awe. Another has called the North Atlantic the "wild ocean." In winter, diabolical gales can rise almost without warning and lash the sea-lanes with 75-mile-an-hour winds and gigantic waves 100 feet from crest to trough. Immense icebergs—small mountains, some of them—break off from the arctic glaciers of Greenland and Iceland and drift disastrously south into the paths of crossing vessels.

Winter on the North Atlantic can last for five months. But in the rest of the year there is scant respite, for the iceberg menace lasts well into summer, and on this ocean, fearsome gales can rise at any season. Even the supposedly benign Gulf Stream often provides maritime treachery. "It contains swift, inner currents, like jets. It fluctuates unpredictably and for unknown causes," explains maritime historian Alan Villiers. "The older mariners dreaded it for its vile effect on contrary gales, for when the wind blew against its direction, so great a sea rose, violently and quickly, as could overwhelm their ship and drown them."

Then there are the hurricanes. Villiers vividly describes the deadly cyclonic storms that may sweep into the North Atlantic from the Gulf of Mexico: "The maddened air, beginning a wild and violent circulatory movement within itself, swept round and round, gyrating at a hundred

Hurricane-force winds rip the tops off mountainous swells in mid-Atlantic as the Cunard Line's Queen Elizabeth weathers one of the worst storms of her career in January 1948. Fearful of the head-on pounding his ship was taking, Captain Charles M. Ford slowed the mightly liner to barely five knots while she bucked waves that surged as high as 80 feet above her water line.

knots and more, shrieking and screaming, an unlashed and frightful primeval force hell-bent for destruction." The sailor's doggerel posted the hurricane season:

July, stand by. August, you must.
September, remember. October, all over.
Then back to "Winter-North Atlantic" once again.

In a small volume titled *Ocean Notes for Ladies,* published in 1877, a British social arbiter named Katherine Ledoux recommended etiquette for those crossing the North Atlantic and for those seeing them off. It echoes the dread the ocean could inspire: "Do not sadden others who are trying hard to be brave too. Leave yourself and them in God's hands, for He will be with you and them, though the trackless deep lies between."

Divine presence, however, was never enough. No one knows how many vessels perished in the North Atlantic in the century after the *Royal William*'s crossing, but there were hundreds upon hundreds of them, with a sacrifice of many thousands of lives. Great numbers of these lost ships were smashed by storms onto shoals or rocky coasts—the great ocean blizzard of March 1891 tossed 15 ships onto the Cornish coast—including the steamship *Marana,* with the loss of all 22 aboard.

But many other ships were torn apart by wind and water alone. In the litany of disasters, a few examples suffice to tell the tale. On October 21, 1874, the paddle steamer *Chusan,* 11 days out of Glasgow, was struck by a gale of immense force; 17 were lost. Scarcely a month later, on November 29, the iron-screw steamer *La Plata,* two days out of Woolwich, was battered to pieces by a full gale; 68 drowned. On December 1, 1879, the emigrant steamer *Borussia,* with 184 settlers and crew, was shattered by a gale; all lifeboats were reduced to kindling except two, in which only 15 souls survived. And on October 19, 1881, the steamer *Clan Macduff,* with 19 passengers and 46 crew, was swamped in a violent storm off Holyhead, and 32 drowned as waves smashed their lifeboats.

Within two weeks in February 1883, both the steamship *Glamorgan* out of Liverpool and the steamship *Kenmure Castle* out of London were torn to pieces by vicious gales. Plowing through a heavy midnight sea, the 320-foot *Glamorgan* was totally submerged by one tremendous wave that swept away her foremast, bridge, all deckhouses, the captain and seven crewmen; staved in her main hatches; and flooded her engine room. Her 44 survivors were rescued just as the hulk plunged down. As for the *Kenmure Castle,* heavy seas tore away her steering gear, crushed her passenger saloon, ripped off the entire superstructure and dragged her to the bottom so fast that only one lifeboat with 16 souls got away; 32 were lost. And so it went, year after year, tempest after tempest.

The ships grew bigger and the odds grew better, but no amount of marble, gilt and plush could quite conceal the ancient, immemorial risks. No amount of horsepower, no leviathan weight of steel could bring a steamer into scale with the Atlantic. "A few more thousand tons," a marine engineer once remarked, "does not intimidate the ocean."

The Cunard Line's *Carmania,* launched in 1905 and the immediate predecessor of the *Lusitania,* had the reputation of being one of the steadiest ships of her day. She was a 19,650-ton giant capable of carrying

After a fierce midwinter storm in 1895 the bridge of the Cunarder Umbria towers like a stately ice palace above her New York dock while passengers and crew marvel at the ship's spectacular frosting. It was a perilous beauty. Around the turn of the century, ice so encumbered a vessel near the coast of Nova Scotia—clogging her winches and steering mechanism, enshrouding the bridge and even freezing her steam whistle—that the captain had to anchor for 12 hours until the storm cleared.

more than 2,600 passengers, requiring 5,000 tons of coal to fuel a voyage from Liverpool to New York and back. Yet on January 4, 1912, an Atlantic storm smashed her lifeboats, tore chairs in the dining room from their mountings and catapulted beds through bulkheads from one stateroom into the next as the ship rolled madly to 50°.

The Cunarder *Aquitania,* even bigger at 45,650 tons and several years more modern, met the North Atlantic at full boil one winter day in 1927. A young officer named Donald MacLean described the encounter:

"I can remember making for the western approaches to the English Channel with a vicious quarterly sea running almost level with the taffrail. It was a tough passage and the *Aquitania* suddenly broached to. As we stood on the wing of the bridge we could hear the ominous crash of the ship's gear being pounded and smashed. When I inspected the boat deck with the Boatswain shortly afterwards we found that three lifeboats had been smashed beyond repair. Down below in the after-cabin dining-saloon every electric circuit was out of action, and the cold green Atlantic was cascading in through sixteen broken ports. The sea washed over the table tops as the ship lurched drunkenly. I was trying to upend a dislodged rack of crockery in the saloon pantry when I heard a groan from one corner. When I shone my flashlight towards the noise all I could see was a face, bleeding profusely, in between the rack battens. I dragged the man to his feet and found it was Old Joe, our night pantryman." As MacLean tried to help Old Joe he discovered to his horror that the man's right eye-socket was empty. "That's all right, sir," Joe said. "It was only a glass 'un."

The Atlantic not only overwhelmed its victims. It could destroy them with subtlety—with impenetrable rain, snow and above all fog, turning navigation into a terrifying game of blindman's buff.

The International Regulations for Preventing Collisions at Sea, often called the Rule of the Road and agreed upon at an international conference in 1890, stated specifically in rule 16: "Every vessel shall, in fog, mist, falling snow, heavy rainstorms or any other conditions similarly restricting visibility, go at a moderate speed, having careful regard to the existing circumstances and conditions." Moderate speed was defined as the speed that would allow a vessel to come to a dead stop in half the distance of existing visibility.

But that was ridiculous if schedules were to be met. Almost universal practice was to pay lip service to the pieties of safety first while heading for port and the Blue Riband at near-full speed.

Samuel Cunard had stated as his governing philosophy: "Speed is nothing. Deliver her safe, bring her back safe—safety is all that is required." And the Cunard Line, above all lines, had an enviable record for protecting passengers from harm. Yet Geoffrey Marr, who rose to become Commodore of the Cunard Line, confessed that "captains and senior officers were prepared to gamble their professional reputations on the mathematical improbability of two ships arriving at the same spot on this large ocean at the same time." And because a captain's reputation, both with his passengers and with his employees, depended largely upon bringing in his ship on time, the practice (as opposed to the theory of rule 16) was to post extra lookouts, close the watertight doors—and slow down the engines very, very marginally.

A ship stranded in fog was like a blind man tapping down a strange road at midnight. The captain would take up more or less permanent residence on the bridge until the fog lifted, stretching his ears, his intuitions and, if he was a God-fearing man, his prayers to pick up signs of another presence. Commodore Bertram Hayes once spent 69 straight fogbound hours in the wheelhouse of the White Star liner *Majestic*. On the *Aquitania*, the last of the four-funnel liners, the convenient method of measuring the fog was to check how many funnels were visible from the bridge. It then became a four-funnel, a three-funnel or—hang out the rabbit's foot—a two-funnel fog.

On the foggy night of Friday, January 22, 1909, two vessels tap-tapped toward each other like blind men, counting as always on the vastness of the Atlantic and the improbability of more than one ship occupying the same space at the same time. It was after midnight before Jack Binns, radio operator on the White Star Line's *Republic*, finished receiving the "Bon voyage" messages and transmitting the "Goodbyes for now" that went with a first-day's sailing from New York; aboard were 461 passengers bound for Genoa and Alexandria. His long day's work done, Binns—a slightly tousled man who looked a bit sleepy even in his normal state—headed straight for his bunk. He slept the virtuous sleep of the seaman who had done his duty—until about 5:30, when he became aware of an increase in horn blasts, then the most chilling of silences at sea. The engines had stopped. No familiar sound, no familiar vibration; it was as if the ship were holding its breath. Then, just after the engines started again, there came a crash like the end of the world.

The *Florida*, a small vessel of the Lloyd Italiano Line, carrying 830 emigrants from Naples to New York, had slammed head on into the port side of the *Republic*. One of the officers of the *Republic* described the collision: "At 5:47 A.M. we heard a whistle about three to four points on our port bow." At that, said the officer, the helm "was immediately put hard-a-port, and the engines run 'stop' and then 'full speed astern.' The engines had been going full astern for two minutes when I saw a vessel. I saw her masthead light on our port beam, and could see by the direction of her lights that she was coming round at a great speed on her starboard helm. She struck us a right-angle blow in the engine room. From the impact I thought that she was going right through us, and as I saw her penetrate further and further into us, I thought that we might float for about three minutes but apparently the *Florida* was a very weak-built ship, and her bows simply crumpled up."

Two seamen on the *Florida* died instantly in the forecastle, which had been turned into a battering-ram. Two passengers on board the *Republic* were crushed to death in their berths; a third was injured and would die a short time later.

The *Florida* ground along the flank of the *Republic*, broke free and disappeared into the fog. Thirty feet of her bow was smashed back, but her collision bulkhead held. Her engine room was undamaged and she was still maneuverable.

But the *Republic* was doomed. Her engine-room wall was raggedly pierced as if by a dull can opener. Her black gang raced frantically for the ladder as the ocean poured in. One man kept his head. If the boilers remained at full pressure until the cold sea hit them, they would almost certainly explode and blow up the *Republic* with them. Fourth Engineer J. G. Legg had the presence of mind to turn on the injector valves before scrambling to safety, thus admitting cold water gradually and lowering the boiler pressure at a safe rate.

While Legg was averting a cataclysm, Binns was dashing to his radio shack, the next compartment to the one where he bunked. The outside bulkhead had been torn away. Twisted metal hung over Binns's head like a canopy. If the *Florida* had struck just a few feet to the right, the smashed bulkhead would have been the one next to his bunk.

Binns threw the switch, touched his key and got a spark. The radio was in working order. But scarcely had he finished his inspection when the power went off and the ship was plunged into darkness; the Atlantic already had flooded the generators. Binns switched to storage batteries. "The bitter cold came inside," he recalled. "I could see nothing outside in the fog and darkness."

Binns's assumption was that the *Republic* had run aground, smashing herself against a rock: "I had no idea as to how badly our ship had been wounded or how long she might remain afloat. The telephone to the bridge had been destroyed by the collision so I was unable to get any details as to the ship's condition."

The radioman and his equipment, now that the engines were gone, were the heart of the ship, and the captain was not long in checking them out. A steward came seeking information, and Binns decided to report in person. A strange scene confronted him as he groped his way through the darkness. The passengers had gathered near the bridge—some of them in bare feet and night clothes. The stewards had returned to the darkened cabins to fetch clothing. In the confusion, wardrobes and owners could not easily be united. Everybody ended up wearing everybody else's garments. Not a few women were bundled up in men's trousers. One elderly man wrapped himself with all the dignity he could muster in one of his wife's spare petticoats. Coffee and sandwiches were being served, along with fruit and whiskey. Jokes were being cracked. The fog-enshrouded deck had the atmosphere of a bizarre costume party.

In the center, on the bridge, stood Captain Sealby, a megaphone in his hands, addressing the passengers, assuring them that all would be well. Binns reported that his radio was still working, then hurried back to the set to commence sending: "*Republic* rammed by unknown steamship, 26 miles southwest of Nantucket. Badly in need of assistance."

SOS—three dots, three dashes, three dots in Morse code—had been officially adopted as the radio-call signal indicating distress, just the previous year by most major nations. Although SOS was a simple signal to transmit, CQD—which some said meant "Come quick, danger"—was still in common usage, particularly in the United States. Binns stayed with the older signal.

The radioman on duty at the nearest land station, Siasconset, on the eastern end of Nantucket, was also feeling the chill. He had just thrown a little coal on the fire when he was startled to hear "CQD" crackling out of his headset. With only his batteries for power, Binns had a broadcasting radius of merely 50 to 60 miles. But it was enough.

With his powerful set, the operator at Siasconset relayed the *Republic*'s message out along the air waves. Then he added a plea of his own: "Do utmost to reach her!"

The distress signal was picked up by the French Line ship *Touraine* and the White Star's *Baltic*. The *Baltic* was near Montauk Point, Long Island—about 64 miles from the *Republic*—when she received the relayed message. She immediately began steaming toward the scene and soon was in direct contact. Binns radioed, "I'm on the job, ship sinking, but will stick to the end." The *Baltic* signaled back: "Don't worry, old man, we are bursting our boilers to get to you."

Meanwhile, the damaged but still seaworthy *Florida* had found her way back to the scene of the collision. Captain Angelo Ruspini, the young skipper of the *Florida*, offered to take on the stricken liner's passengers. Within two hours, small boats had transferred the *Republic*'s passengers and all but 45 members of the British ship's 300-man crew. One imperturbable woman passenger played solitaire on the tilting deck of the *Republic* until her turn in the boat came. But now one ship, with a makeshift canvas patch on what was left of her bow, was perilously overloaded, and the other ship was steadily sinking.

By noon the transfer to the *Florida* was completed. And by then, Binns recollected, "the *Baltic* was within 10 miles of us; I could tell by the strength of her signals." But the fog was getting even thicker.

For six desperate hours the *Baltic* circled, trying to find the *Republic*. The two ships blew their foghorns, detonated rockets, exploded signal bombs. Binns tapped out messages. The sending lever had broken off; Binns had to hold down the key that closed the circuit with one hand while transmitting with the other. All he could see from his ruined shack were the canvas-covered bodies of the *Republic*'s dead on the boat deck. To keep from freezing, to keep from feeling he was the last, lonely man on earth, Binns carried a message in person to the bridge. "My teeth rattled and I was scarcely able to talk," he remembered. Captain Sealby, mistaking chill for fear, felt obliged to reassure his radioman that everything would turn out right.

At 6 p.m. the words rang hollow. The ship was sinking by the head. Darkness was descending. The *Baltic* was still out there somewhere circling in the dense fog, and now the *Republic* had lost sight of the *Florida*. All the rockets had been detonated on both the *Republic* and the *Baltic*. Each ship was down to her last signal bomb. The two vessels compared their chronometers by radio. At a given second the *Republic* exploded her last bomb. The *Baltic* heard nothing. Now it was the *Baltic*'s turn—the last turn.

On the bridge of the *Republic* the quartermaster stood by the chronometer, ready to signal the precise moment when the *Baltic* was scheduled to explode her final bomb. The 44 other men left on the *Republic* stood in a circle, silent, motionless, facing all points of the compass, as if in a primitive ritual of prayer.

The quartermaster gave the signal—"Now!"—and the men in the circle listened as they had never listened before. Binns and the third officer,

Radio operator Jack Binns stands relaxed and smiling after orchestrating the epic sea rescue of some 1,650 passengers and crewmen when his White Star liner Republic collided with the small Italian vessel Florida in fog off Nantucket in 1909. Binns transmitted more than 200 signals during a 36-hour vigil on board the sinking Republic.

With a tattered canvas spread over the jagged wreckage of her bow, the Florida limps into New York Harbor two days after she collided with the Republic. Despite heavy damage, the liner returned to New York under her own power—arriving with flags at half-mast in honor of the two Florida crew members and three Republic passengers who died in the tragic mishap.

standing next to him, heard, or thought they heard, the faintest of booms. Binns rushed back to his radio to signal directions. Fifteen minutes later the men on the *Republic* heard a foghorn. Now Binns began to guide the *Baltic* to him: "You are on the port bow. . . . Now you are dead ahead. . . . You are coming too close. . . . Back away or you will ram us."

Ten minutes later, Binns heard a great cheer erupt in the darkness and fog: "I knew, of course, it could not come from our crew, as we were only about 45." He peered out through his cabin door: "There was the *Baltic*, alongside of us. She was a magnificent and inspiring sight; ablaze with light from every port; all the passengers were lining the rail cheering."

Suddenly the fog lifted. The weather shifted to cold, driving rain. The *Florida* was sighted again. The *Republic* was abandoned, but hope for her was not abandoned. Anything began to seem possible now. As if keeping vigil, Captain Sealby and a boat crew circled the sinking ship all night while a second major operation was going on. The captains had decided that all *Republic* and *Florida* passengers, together with most of the *Republic* crew, should be transferred from the damaged and overloaded *Florida* to the *Baltic*. It was the greatest open-sea maneuver of its kind in history. About 1,650 men, women and children were involved. Conditions were far from ideal. It was nighttime—the transferring did not even get under way until 11:30 p.m. There was a strong wind, with long, rolling swells. The rain continued.

Two women, descending into the small boats, lost their footing and fell into the sea. They were quickly hauled out with no worse effect than an icy drenching.

The women and children came first. Then the first-class male passengers of the *Republic*. The male emigrants of the *Florida* protested: "There are no classes here, we are all equal." Their argument was lost on the officers of the *Republic* and the *Baltic*, conditioned to acknowledge social privilege even in a small boat on a roiling ocean.

The last boatload reached the *Baltic* at about 7 a.m. Daylight found a flotilla of would-be rescuers drawn to the scene by Binns's CQD: passenger steamers, graceful revenue cutters and stodgy freighters.

As the nautical congregation watched, Captain Sealby and a skeleton crew, including the indefatigable Binns, returned to the still-sinking *Republic*. Sealby, reassuming his position on the bridge, now thought that he could save his ship by beaching her on a shelf of shallow water. Nailing up blankets over his well-ventilated shack, Binns stood by his radio. As the *Baltic* passed close to the *Republic* and set out for New York, a huzzah went up for the faithful remnant of crew manning the *Republic*. The *Florida* plodded slowly after the *Baltic*, a canvas patch covering her crumpled bow.

Then the revenue cutter *Gresham* attached a steel hawser to the *Republic* to tow her, while the Anchor Line's *Furnessia* made fast to the stern to act as a rudder. But the *Gresham*—even when joined in the tow by the Navy destroyer *Seneca*—could make very little headway. As night fell, water seeped into Binns's cabin. At last the captain gave the order to abandon ship. Binns's final message read: "Current going, wireless now closed."

Everybody left in the captain's gig, rowing to the *Gresham*—except Captain Sealby, who refused to abandon his sinking ship while she still floated, and Second Officer Williams, selected for the hazardous honor of remaining with the captain because he was the senior unmarried man. The steel towing hawser was replaced by a manila rope, and a sailor with an ax was stationed on the *Gresham*'s stern to cut the *Republic* loose when she went down. Of the ships gathered in the morning, four or five still remained, playing their searchlights on the final act. Sealby and Williams could be clearly seen, pacing up and down the bridge.

Soon the taffrail was awash, with only the flagpole and the British ensign above water there. At 8:30 p.m., almost 39 hours after the collision, Sealby and Williams set off blue flares. To help attract attention, Sealby also fired five shots from his revolver. Then both men climbed down the ladder from the bridge to the saloon deck. Sealby recalled: "The deck was wet and slippery with a 30-degree list making it impossible for us to keep on our feet, so we grabbed the rail and crawled along. The explosions of the air driven out by water and the rending of frames amidships told us that the stern was already under water. I managed to get the foremast and climbed the rigging as far as the running light about 100 feet up. Below me half the ship was visible and she tipped up like a rocking chair about to go over backward.

"My blue light would not burn because it was wet, so I fired the last shot from my revolver. Then everything dropped and I was in the water

Under clear skies and in benign seas, the Titanic skirts the south coast of Ireland, steaming gracefully out of home waters for the first—and last—time on April 11, 1912. On board, as an unknown photographer on shore snapped this picture, were 2,206 passengers and crew members, sharing a rare sense of confidence and privilege as participants in the maiden voyage of the newest, largest and most luxurious ship in the world.

with the foremast slipping down beside me like an elevator plunger. There was a boiling, seething mass of water about me and a great roaring noise. I went under, but bobbed up again immediately as the air under my great coat buoyed me up.''

The *Republic* sank at 8:40. Captain Sealby managed to catch a spar, then a hatch cover. Wreckage eddied all around him. He pulled himself partway up on the hatch cover, out of the way of the whirling debris. Still, only his head and shoulders were above water. The sea was icy cold. He could see the *Gresham*'s lights sweeping the water. Numbly he slipped another cartridge into his revolver and pulled the trigger. Rather to his surprise the gun went off. A search boat heard the shot and fished him out. Williams was found nearby. Both men were exhausted.

In New York, Sealby received a tremendous ovation from the crowd of 3,000 or more that greeted the survivors at White Star's pier. But Jack Binns, to his surprise, and rather to his horror, found himself the unofficial hero, raised on the shoulders of the crowd, kissed by clerks in the White Star office. Vaudeville offers besieged him.

The following evening a dinner was given in his honor. Afterward, by a press agent's guile, the innocent Binns was lured to the Hippodrome to see the water ballet. After the performance the spotlight was thrown on Binns in his box, and the Hippodrome manager announced: "CQD Binns is in the house." The confused and outraged Binns was half-dragged to the stage and forced to acknowledge a standing ovation. As soon as the curtain fell, a massed formation of 50 or more water ballerinas rushed to kiss him. Binns fled down into the basement and hid in the elephant stalls of the old circus building.

Back in England, adulation was equally burdensome. In Binns's native town of Peterborough, the mayor, local dignitaries in state robes and most of his fellow townsmen greeted him at the station and escorted him to the guildhall, where there were more speeches.

The enshrinement of Binns as a popular idol was understandable. Radio was the new magic, and the man who could control it was the new wizard. The so-called wireless had been introduced on board transatlantic commercial liners only a decade before with the *Kaiser Wilhelm der Grosse*. The rescue of the passengers of the *Republic* and the *Florida*—with Binns's radio pulling in ships like a magnet—was the first demonstration of this new lifesaving machine. Fate and the Atlantic Ocean had been cheated. In the ongoing battle of the Age of Technology, who could doubt after this near-disaster that Science was triumphing over Nature?

On Sunday morning, April 14, 1912, the White Star flagship *Titanic* was four days out of Southampton, proceeding at 22 1/2 knots toward completion of what promised to be a triumphant maiden voyage. The air was clear, the sea glass-calm. As if daunted by this newest presence, the Atlantic was on its best behavior. "The sea is like a millpond," one passenger wrote his wife. Another passenger recalled: "There was nothing to indicate or suggest that we were on the stormy Atlantic Ocean. The motion of the ship and the noise of its machinery were scarcely discernible on deck or in the saloons, either day or night." A veteran stoker on the crew could not remember a calmer sea in 26 years.

But although it was spring, the air was chill on the North Atlantic sea-lanes. And all day long, Captain E. J. Smith, 59, a quiet man with shaggy eyebrows, received wireless messages—from the French liner *Touraine*, from the German liner *Amerika*—warning of icebergs ahead in the path of the *Titanic*. Smith, starting out in sail, had earned his master's certificate at the age of 25 and had served 32 years with White Star. He was known as a prudent, experienced seaman. Yet although he acknowledged the repeated and urgent warnings, and sent a lookout aloft to watch for the bergs, he took no further action. "I cannot imagine any condition which would cause a ship to founder," he had remarked some years before. "Modern shipbuilding has gone beyond that." As for the *Titanic*, she had been designed with every advance in mind; with her double bottom and 16 automatically controlled watertight compartments, she was considered unsinkable.

At 11:40 that night, while the captain was in his cabin, lookout Frederick Fleet, high in the crow's-nest of this most invulnerable of ships, saw an object directly ahead that was neither starlit sky nor black water. At first the object looked small. But second by second it grew larger. Quickly, Fleet banged the crow's-nest bell three times, the danger signal, and lifted the phone to call the bridge.

"What did you see?" a disinterested voice asked at the other end.

"Iceberg right ahead," Fleet answered.

"Thank you," the voice acknowledged.

For half a minute, Fleet watched the iceberg draw nearer, as if it and not the ship were moving, and still the *Titanic* did not turn. Now the two floating objects were almost together. Fleet looked up at the iceberg, towering wet and shiny above the forecastle deck, and braced himself for the crash. Then, at last, the bow began to swing to port into clear water. The iceberg glided by along the starboard side. Near-miss. Or so Fleet thought.

Quartermaster George Rowe, standing watch on the after bridge, felt a jolt, a break in rhythm. Glancing forward, he saw what looked like a ghostly windjammer coming toward him, sails set. He realized it was an iceberg, looming perhaps 100 feet above the water. Then, as swiftly as it had appeared, it vanished in the dark.

In the galley the chief night baker, Walter Belford, was making rolls for the following day. This small jolt knocked a pan of new rolls off the top of the oven and scattered them about the floor.

Indeed, Mrs. John Jacob Astor, lying in her suite's bedroom, thought this tiniest of disturbances registered a mishap in the kitchen. Lady Cosmo Duff Gordon, waking up in her bed, compared the tremor to a giant finger being drawn along the side of the ship.

In the smoking room a game of cards was in progress, with several onlookers. One had seen an iceberg through the windows. He called it to the attention of his companions. Nobody was sufficiently interested to go on deck. The game went on. One of the players, pointing to his glass of whiskey, turned to one of the bystanders and said: "Just run along the deck and see if any ice has come aboard. I would like some for this." There was general laughter.

The engines stopped. When it was discovered that an iceberg had been sighted, one wag suggested: "I expect the iceberg has scratched off some of her new paint, and the Captain doesn't like to go on until she is painted up again."

In fact, Captain Smith had rushed to the bridge from his cabin next to the wheelhouse when he felt the jolt.

A sheet from the radio operator's pad on the Russian steamer Birma records the Titanic's call for help: "CQD—SOS from MGY. We have struck iceberg. Sinking fast. Come to our assistance." CQD was the original Morse code distress signal. It was replaced in 1908 by the more comprehensible SOS. The Titanic's operator, using both, began broadcasting the first SOS messages at 12:45 a.m.; the Birma—100 miles west and in another time zone—logged this one in at 11:50.

"Mr. Murdoch, what was that?" he asked the officer on watch.

"An iceberg, sir. I hard-a-starboarded and reversed the engines, and I was going to hard-a-port around it, but she was too close. I couldn't do any more."

"Close the emergency doors."

"The doors are already closed."

J. Bruce Ismay, Chairman of the White Star Line, had wakened with a start in his deluxe suite on B deck when the *Titanic* brushed the iceberg. Putting on his carpet slippers and pulling a suit over his pajamas, he had padded up to the bridge to find out what was happening.

"Do you think the ship is seriously damaged?" Ismay asked when told of the iceberg.

Captain Smith slowly answered, "I'm afraid she is," as if trying to digest the news himself. He had just received his first report from the ship's carpenter, who had informed him: "She's making water fast!"

Thomas Andrews, managing director of Harland & Wolff Shipyard, builders of the *Titanic,* barely noticed the jolt. All day long he had roamed the ship, cheerfully attending to minor chores, graciously accepting a special loaf of bread the chief baker had created in his honor, and taking voluminous notes: Trouble with the restaurant galley. Wrong coloring for the dashing on the promenade decks—too dark.

When the *Titanic* so gently jostled at lat. 41° 46′ N., long. 50° 14′ W., her builder was totally absorbed in a blueprint of the writing room. It was simply too large, so Andrews had decided to subdivide half of it into two deluxe staterooms. He had barely noticed the tremor when he received Captain Smith's message asking him to report to the bridge.

Andrews and the captain made their tour of the ship down the crew's stairway, hoping not to attract attention. Andrews understood ships, one admirer said, the way some men understood horses. The two men passed the squash court, where water already lapped against the foul line on the backboard. They passed the mail room, where the sea was surging in.

Andrews put together his data. That kiss from the iceberg had ripped a 300-foot gash down the starboard side of the *Titanic,* slicing through her thick plates as though they were butter. In scarcely 10 minutes, water had flooded into the first five compartments up to 14 feet—the forepeak, No. 1 hold, No. 2 hold, No. 5 boiler room, No. 6 boiler room.

And here the jolt had not been cushioned, as it was topside. In boiler room No. 5 the impact had knocked the firemen off their feet and buried one hapless soul under an avalanche of coal from the bunkers. As they had scrambled upright, the men had faced a jet of sea water pouring in through a two-foot gash.

To Captain Smith, Andrews explained what all this meant. The first four compartments could be flooded, and the *Titanic* would still float. But the bulkhead between the fifth and sixth compartments went only as high as E deck. When the water from the fifth compartment reached this point, it would spill over into the sixth compartment. When the sixth compartment flooded, the water would spill over into the seventh compartment, and so on. There was a total of 16 compartments, but already the *Titanic* was doomed. Andrews gave the *Titanic* an hour, perhaps an hour and a half, to live.

Tragic farewells on the Titanic's lifeboat deck are depicted in a 1912 illustration from The Sphere. At left, a young husband urges his wife to join other women in the boats. Someone has lost a shoe in his haste, and a tuxedo-clad passenger carelessly holding his life vest blows a last kiss to his wife as crewmen drag her to the boats. At right, queues of passengers await instructions, some grim, some weeping.

A cutaway illustration from a 1912 issue of the British periodical The Sphere shows why upper-deck passengers failed to grasp the seriousness of the Titanic's plight. To them the ship appeared only to have sideswiped the iceberg; they saw no serious damage. Crewmen and passengers who were far below and on the starboard side, however, knew better. A tremendous crash sent some tumbling out of their bunks. The ice had gashed a 300-foot slit in the ship, letting in a torrent of water.

First Class | Lounge | Promenade

Corridor | Private Suite | Promenade

Bath Rooms

ICEBERG
From 50 to 100 feet
according to various
accounts

← Starboard port holes

Water Line

Boiler Room

At 12:05 a.m. Captain Smith ordered the lifeboats uncovered. Then he stuck his head in the radio shack and told first operator John George Phillips: "Send the call for assistance."

Phillips began tapping out the message, repeated six times.

A few passengers noticed that the ship was not perfectly level. The commutator on the bridge showed the *Titanic* slightly down at the head and listing 5° to starboard. She was already more than a quarter sunk, but only the captain, Andrews and a very few others were aware of the real situation. Least aware of all were the first-class passengers. "You don't catch me leaving a warm bed to go up on that cold deck at midnight," one passenger told friends, and the same attitude prevailed even after the call went up: "All passengers on deck with lifebelts on."

On the boat deck the first-class and second-class passengers assembled casually, unhurriedly. The *Titanic* lay in utter repose—not even rocking to the gentle swell of the sea. "To stand on the deck many feet above the water lapping idly against her sides," a passenger remembered, "gave one a sense of wonderful security: to feel her so steady and still was like standing on a large rock in the middle of the ocean." There was remarkably little conversation—and what there was was not excited. The scene seemed likely to turn into a still life under a brilliantly beautiful starlit night.

Belowdecks, stewards were engaged in locking staterooms to ensure that nothing would be stolen from them during their occupants' temporary absence. One man somehow locked himself in his cabin. His shouts and bangings attracted passengers a little tardy in getting topside. One of them, more amused than concerned, broke down the door. The head steward appeared and was so furious when he saw the damage that he threatened the door crasher with arrest in New York, for destroying property of the White Star Line.

As passengers gathered topside, the boilers' safety valves blew off steam. In the clouds of vapor the engineer, John Shepherd, tripped and broke his leg. Assistant Engineer Herbert Harvey and two firemen had carried Shepherd to the pump room when the flooding, just as Andrews had predicted, reached E-deck level and spilled over. The bulkhead between boiler room No. 5 and boiler room No. 6 collapsed under the pressure of the inrushing water. Harvey shouted to fireman Fred Barrett to make for the escape ladder. The last Barrett saw of Harvey, he was heading toward the injured Shepherd. Then he disappeared under a foaming torrent of water.

The passengers, watching the steam issue out of a pipe extending high up one of the funnels—"a harsh deafening boom"—could hardly know how deadly a signal it was. Above the noise of escaping steam, an officer dressed casually with a white muffler twisted around his neck ordered: "All women and children get down to deck below, and all men stand back from the boats."

There had been no boat drill, and things went awkwardly. The crew put in lanterns and tins of biscuits at this last minute. Ropes were uncoiled. Cranks were inserted in the davits, then turned. Davits groaned, pulleys shrilled and slowly each boat was lowered. With one foot in No. 6 boat and one foot on the deck, Second Officer Charles Lightoller called for women and children. The response was not enthusiastic. John Jacob Astor spoke for all when he declared: "We are safer here than in that little boat." As one woman climbed into her boat, a friend called: "When you get back you'll need a pass. You can't get back on tomorrow morning without a pass."

The steerage passengers were not under the illusions of the higher-class passengers. For those on the starboard side the collision had been no faint jar but a tremendous blow that had catapulted them out of bed. Within 10 minutes of the impact, even those on the portside looked out of their bunks and found an inch or two of water swirling on deck. At the foot of the main steerage staircase on E deck, passengers soon appeared, carrying boxes, bags and trunks aft like refugees in wartime. There were Swedes, Norwegians, Danes, Finns, Poles, Russians, Dutchmen, Spaniards, Italians, Rumanians, Greeks, Arabs and even Chinese.

Seamen stood behind locked gates at points leading up from the third-class decks to prevent steerage passengers from gaining access to the upper decks. Even in disaster, class distinctions prevailed. At one of these barriers, three Irish girls—Kathy Gilnagh, Kate Mullins and Kate Murphy—were turned back from the stairway leading to the upper decks. Jim Farrell, a lad from the girls' home country, made his way up to the barrier and bellowed, "Great God, man! Open the gate and let the girls through!" The sailor meekly obeyed.

Others managed to break down barriers that were not guarded, or climbed emergency ladders intended only for crew's use and slowly, circuitously made their way topside. Rather like two children lost in the forest, Anna Sjoblom, an 18-year-old Finnish girl, and a companion stumbled up such a ladder and suddenly came upon the brightly lit first-class à-la-carte French restaurant, like an enchanted castle. The girls, spellbound, half-forgot their fears as they pressed their faces to the windows and stared at the rose-colored carpet, the pink-shaded table lamps, set with silver and crystal and china for the next day.

But most of the steerage passengers milled from barrier to barrier, some ending up back in their cabins, or congregated in the third-class dining saloon clutching their rosaries in their hands. With what they knew firsthand—E deck forward was waist-deep in water—third-class passengers would not have needed any coaxing to enter the lifeboats. But the cruel facts stood thus: 2,206 people were on board the *Titanic*; there were 16 wooden lifeboats and four canvas collapsible lifeboats, with a total capacity of 1,178. Nearly half of the passengers on the *Titanic* had no place to go.

Still, there was hope. The night air crackled with radio signals. Phillips tapped a signal to the Cunarder *Carpathia*: "CQD CQD SOS SOS CQD SOS. Come at once. We have struck a berg. Position 41.46° N., 50.14° W. CQD SOS." The reply crackled through Phillips' earphones—the *Carpathia* was only 58 miles away and "coming hard."

Even more promising was the light that Fourth Officer Joseph Boxhall spotted 10 miles off the *Titanic*'s bow. Binoculars showed the outline of a steamer. Boxhall tried to signal with the Morse lamp. He thought he got an answer but could not read it and decided he was seeing the ship's mast light flickering.

A last rocket flares up as the crew of the
doomed Titanic prepares to abandon ship.
In this dramatic sketch, made by
steward Leo James Hyland after his rescue,
the Titanic's forecastlehead is already
underwater, the well deck is flooding and
the bridge is imperiled as the last
of the lifeboats are lowered into the
sea. Passengers clustered on the
stern hold fast to the railings to keep from
sliding forward on the angled deck.

At about 12:45 Captain Smith asked for signal rockets. Lawrence Beesley, a young science master at Dulwich College, traveling second class, recollected that there was "suddenly a rush of light from the forward deck, a hissing roar that made us all turn from watching the boats, and a rocket leapt upwards to where the stars blinked and twinkled above us. Up it went, higher and higher, with a sea of faces upturned to watch it, and then an explosion that seemed to split the silent night in two, and a shower of stars sank slowly down and went out one by one. And with a gasping sigh one word escaped the lips of the crowd: 'Rockets!' Anybody knows what rockets at sea mean. We were calling for help from any one who was near enough to see."

Only 19 miles away the Leyland liner *Californian*, quite probably the vessel Boxhall had sighted, had prudently halted for the night upon encountering icebergs. Her radio was shut down at 11:30 when the only wireless operator aboard went off duty. On her bridge the officer on watch saw the sudden blaze of light above the strange, motionless steamer and wondered why in the world this apparently undistressed ship would fire rockets in the middle of the night. If he could have heard across the miles of water, he would have been even more mystified. At about this time the cellist from the *Titanic* band came around the corner of the starboard boat deck and ran aft, his cello trailing behind him, the spike dragging along the deck. In the first-class lounge he was joined by the seven other members of the ship's band, some dressed in their blue uniforms. Soon the sounds of music—"Great Big Beautiful Doll," "Alexander's Ragtime Band"—mingled with the sounds of boats being lowered into the water.

One by one the lifeboats descended into the sea: No. 6 at 12:55, No. 3 at 1 o'clock, No. 8 at 1:10. As the deck became more and more a male province, the husbands smoked, drifted down into the lounge or settled in wicker chairs in the gymnasium, where the electric horse, electric camel and stationary bicycles stood riderless and idle.

No. 8 boat held the first of the steerage women and children to be accommodated. By then No. 1 boat had already been lowered with five passengers, six stokers and a lookout on board—12 people in a boat designed to hold 40.

One more group from steerage was escorted to No. 15 boat, which embarked at about 1:30. A wave of men from steerage rushed both No. 14 and No. 15, but they were beaten back, in one case by a seaman swinging a tiller as a club, in another case by warning shots from an officer's pistol. At 1:55, No. 4 boat, the last of the wooden lifeboats, was lowered into the sea—just 15 feet below now.

For over an hour the *Titanic*'s builder, Thomas Andrews, had walked from boat to boat, urging the women to hurry: "Ladies, you *must* get in at once. There is not a moment to lose. You cannot pick and choose your boat." When he had done all he could, he retreated to the smoking room. A steward discovered him there, standing alone. His life belt was tossed carelessly across the top of a table. His arms were folded. He was looking at a painting. Its title was *The Approach of the New World*. The steward said to him, "Aren't you going to have a try for it, Mr. Andrews?" Andrews did not speak, or even move.

Terrified and half-frozen after a night of horror among the icebergs, a boatload of survivors from the Titanic nestles at dawn alongside the rescue vessel Carpathia. Above them, doors have been opened in the ship's side and a rope boarding ladder has been lowered.

The heroine of the Titanic tragedy (shown here in an early picture) was a spunky Denver millionairess, Molly Brown. Adrift in a lifeboat with 22 other women and five men, she took command when the men panicked, organized the women to row, and also brought another lifeboat with 56 survivors under her wing. They were saved by the Carpathia, and Molly graciously rewarded the crew by having medals struck for each member. She was ever after known as the "Unsinkable Molly Brown."

The *Titanic* had entered upon her death throes. The lights were now dulled, burning with a reddish tinge. Most of the staterooms were flooded, even the *suites de luxe* on C deck. As water began washing over the boat deck, the little band abandoned popular tunes and began to play the hymn "Autumn."

On the *Californian* it looked to the officer on watch as if the strange ship's lowering position on the horizon meant she was sailing away. He ordered a young apprentice to awaken his captain and inform him that an unidentified ship was disappearing to the southwest and that she had fired, in all, eight rockets. The captain's only question was: "Were they all white?" The answer was yes. The captain rolled over and went back to sleep—thereby stirring a controversy that has raged ever since. Why had he not responded? Was it because the vessel was reported steaming away? Was he loath to risk his own ship among the icebergs? Or was he simply befuddled by sleep? In any case, he took no action.

The time was 2:10. An estimated 700 passengers and crewmen were in the lifeboats designed to have a capacity of almost 1,200. An estimated 1,500 people were left on the ship. To those in the lifeboats, the *Titanic* still seemed a proud ship commanding an extraordinary authority. The only thing wrong, they recalled, was the "awful angle" at which she rested in the sea. Suddenly the *Titanic* tilted upward until she stood upright, and for a half minute she hung motionless. Her lights went out, came on again for a flash, then went out for good. There was a frightening sound—"partly a roar, partly a groan, partly a rattle," a survivor remembered—as her boilers and engines broke loose from their mountings. When the noise subsided, the *Titanic* was still suspended upright, some 150 feet of her stern jutting out of water.

After perhaps as long as four minutes, she commenced her plunge. Those in the lifeboats braced themselves in expectation of the huge wave that would boil up around them as the ship sank. But there was no wave, only another sound. The presence of the *Titanic*, a survivor wrote, was replaced by "the agonizing cries of death from over a thousand throats, the wails and groans of the suffering, the shrieks of the terror-stricken and the awful gaspings for breath of those in the last throes of drowning." The motionless sea was covered with tangled wreckage and the struggling forms of hundreds of men, women and children.

One by one the voices that made up that chorus died away. The water was a deadly 28° F. Within 40 minutes there was silence. Only one boat, commanded by Fifth Officer Harold Lowe, made an organized attempt to pick up survivors.

At least 13 ships had heard the *Titanic's* distress signal—first a German vessel, the *Frankfort*, then the Cunard liner *Carpathia*. The *Carpathia* was the first to arrive on the scene. Captain Arthur Rostron spotted a green flare on the horizon at 2:35, located about half a point off the port bow. Ten minutes after that the *Carpathia* sighted her first iceberg. Then another and another. Without slowing down, Rostron dodged icebergs on all sides, steering toward the green flares that appeared from time to time. By 4 o'clock the *Carpathia* had arrived at the *Titanic's* radioed position. There was no sign of her. Rostron stopped all engines, but his heart was sinking.

Just then another green flare shot up, outlining a lifeboat perhaps 300 yards ahead. Boat No. 2, under the command of Fourth Officer Joseph Boxhall, pulled toward the *Carpathia*. The life belts made everybody in the boat look to those peering down from the rail as if they were dressed in white. The only sound was that of a baby wailing. At 4:10, Elizabeth Allen climbed slowly up the swinging ladder and fell into the arms of the *Carpathia*'s purser.

In the gray light of dawn, boats could soon be seen, scattered over a four-mile area, almost indistinguishable from scores of small icebergs. Three or four icebergs, 150 to 200 feet high, towered over the rest. To the north and west for five miles or so, a flat, unbroken field of ice floes stretched to the horizon.

In all, 703 survivors were snatched from the sea: 210 out of 898 of the crew, 493 out of 1,308 passengers. Bruce Ismay was saved; Thomas Andrews and Captain Smith went down with their ship. In all, 1,503 lives were lost. It was the greatest disaster since mariners began challenging the Atlantic.

Moralists, like the Bishop of Winchester, saw God's judgment. "When has such a mighty lesson against our confidence and trust in power, machinery, and money been shot through the nation? The *Titanic*, name and thing, will stand for a monument and warning to human presumption." Perhaps. But like the lessons of every other calamity, the lessons of the *Titanic*—the lessons that could never be forgotten—were eventually forgotten.

By the mid-1950s, man's ingenuity and progress had reached new heights on the sea. Virtually every oceangoing vessel carried a radio device called loran that could fix a ship's position within a quarter of a mile by measuring the crisscrossing beams emitted by stations on land hundreds of miles distant. By another technological miracle, radar could penetrate the densest fog or darkest night to paint the outlines of harbors and shores or, most importantly, detect the presence far away of oncoming vessels. Collision at sea need never occur again.

Marine design had advanced as well; soon liners were veritable honeycombs of double bottoms, watertight bulkheads and isolated engine compartments—everything operated by doubly and triply redundant control systems. And yet the liners, mankind's grandest creations, remained as vulnerable as the men who rode their bridges.

On the evening of July 25, 1956, two transatlantic liners with quite different destinations in mind were unsuspectingly racing toward a rendezvous with each other. The Italian liner *Andrea Doria* was speeding west, due in New York at 6 a.m. the following day. The *Stockholm* of the Swedish-American Line had left New York at 11:30 that morning and had shaped a course that would take her east to the Nantucket Lightship and thence across the Atlantic to Europe.

At 2:40 p.m., with the Nantucket Lightship still 165 miles away, a patchy mist was beginning to encircle the *Andrea Doria*. Captain Piero Calamai ordered fog precautions to be taken. At about 3 p.m. the foghorn began to utter its mournful warning at 100-second intervals. The doors connecting the ship's 11 watertight compartments below A deck were

The Titanic's captain, Edward J. Smith, the very picture of a patrician sea dog, met an uncertain death when his vessel went down. He is reported variously to have shot himself, to have yelled through his megaphone, "Be British!"—and even to have swum to a lifeboat, handed a baby aboard, then gallantly moved away when informed there was no room for him.

closed. The lookout in the crow's-nest was sent forward to stand his turn on watch on the peak of the ship's bow. In addition, the engine room was notified, "We're in fog." Steam pressure in the four boilers was reduced from 40 to 37 kilograms per square centimeter, which meant the *Andrea Doria* was proceeding at 21.8 knots instead of 23 knots. The engine telegraphs on the bridge and in the engine room remained set at full speed ahead. And why not?

On the bridge, to the right of the helm, a radar set was switched on to the 20-mile range, and one of the two officers on watch was stationed before this electronic lookout. Anything of any size would appear as a bright yellow blip long before the ship came anywhere near.

Captain Calamai was a responsible mariner, less than two years away from the Italian Line's compulsory retirement age of 60. He had spent 40 years at sea and had served as an officer on 27 ships before being chosen as master of the *Andrea Doria*, 29,100-ton pride of the Italian Line. In the three and a half years since her maiden voyage—50 trips in all—he had been her only captain. His record was unblemished, and the only flaw he was criticized for was his patience. He was too mild, some said—not enough of a disciplinarian.

But on this voyage, Captain Calamai was one hour behind schedule because of a storm two nights before. He had 1,134 passengers aboard who expected, naturally, to reach their destination on time. Back in Genoa, the Italian Line's managers had the same expectation, for different reasons. Tomorrow morning 200 longshoremen would be lining the New York pier to unload 401 tons of freight, nine automobiles, 522 pieces of baggage and 1,754 bags of mail. They would have to be paid whether the *Andrea Doria* arrived or not. In addition, there was the cost of fuel: 10 to 11 tons of oil for every hour the *Andrea Doria* spent at sea— enough to heat an average house for two years.

And so Captain Calamai went to the bridge and rode his luck. Twice the fog cleared briefly. The first time, Captain Calamai returned to his cabin to finish some paper work. The second time, he went below to change from his summer whites to his evening blues; the weather was turning chilly in the fog. As the mists closed in again, he ordered his dinner on the bridge, and then at 8:30 p.m. he settled down to his long night's vigil.

At about the same time, Johan-Ernst Carstens-Johannsen, a young third officer, was taking over the watch on the *Stockholm*, outbound to the Nantucket Lightship, anchored beyond the shoals of Nantucket Island. Captain H. Gunnar Nordenson, 63, with 45 years at sea, was in his cabin. But he was a taskmaster, and his demanding presence could be felt everywhere on a liner the size of the *Stockholm*—12,165 tons and only 525 feet long.

Captain Nordenson allowed no smoking or coffee drinking to divert the attention of officers on the bridge of the *Stockholm*. Conversation on watch was strictly in the line of duty. Officers were forbidden to fraternize with seamen lest discipline break down.

The sky was cloudy and overcast when Carstens came on watch at 8:30. He checked the navigation lights each time he went out on a bridge wing: two white masthead lights, visible for five miles, plus the green

sidelight below the bridge on the starboard side and the red sidelight on
the port side, each visible for two miles. These were the standard running lights, signals in effect for many years, by which one vessel warned
another of its presence and indicated its relative position. A seaman
stood watch in the crow's-nest. The radar was set to 15 miles. Nothing
was visible on the screen.

Around 9 o'clock Captain Nordenson made an appearance. "Call me
when you see Nantucket," he said as he left the wheelhouse. His habit
was to stay awake on the first night until the Nantucket Lightship—now
about 40 miles ahead—was passed and the course changed.

At 10:20 the senior second officer on the *Andrea Doria*, Curzio Franchini, who was manning the radar, called out to Captain Calamai, "We
are abeam of Nantucket. Distance—one mile." As the *Andrea Doria* sped
by the lightship, which was invisible in the fog, Captain Calamai gave
orders for the new course: "Steer 268"—almost due west. The *Andrea
Doria* was on the home leg. And now she became aware that another ship
was traveling her lane.

About 20 minutes after passing the Nantucket Lightship, Franchini
observed a small, barely perceptible blip at the edge of his radarscope. At
first he thought it was a ship the *Andrea Doria* was overtaking. When he
realized the blip was a ship coming toward him, he notified Captain
Calamai. By that time the blip was 17 miles away, 4° to starboard. Franchini followed the blip as it came closer, applying the rule of thumb: if
the angle of bearing increases, a safe passing will occur.

Two hypotheses were assumed. Franchini thought the angle was, in
fact, increasing. Captain Calamai thought the other vessel was a fishing
trawler heading for Nantucket Island. The Rule of the Road requires
ships meeting head on to turn right for a port-to-port passing. Entertain-
ing his fishing-trawler premise, Captain Calamai preferred to turn left, if
necessary, toward the open sea rather than toward land and shoals. He
was confident that he had room for a starboard-to-starboard passing.

At about 10:50 a blip appeared on the screen of the *Stockholm*, about
12 miles away. When the distance was reduced to 10 miles, Carstens
decided to plot it. The blip at that moment was 2° to port. Just as the
bridge clock rang six bells for 11 p.m., Carstens plotted the blip at six
miles and 4° to port. He drew a line between his two fixes and computed
that the other vessel would pass the *Stockholm* about one half to one
mile to port, in accordance with the Rule of the Road. Long before then,
Carstens expected to see the other ship, for the *Stockholm* had not yet
run into even the smallest patch of fog. When, at 11:03, the radarscope
showed the other ship to be only four miles away, Carstens assumed that
her lights were defective, or else that she was a Naval vessel on maneu-
vers and blacked out. He did not dream that a thick, light-dimming fog
had set in just a few thousand feet away. Had he even suspected fog, he
would have immediately called Captain Nordenson, who was busy writing in his personal diary: "Beautiful weather and warm, a slight haze on
the horizon. 1131 departed from New York. It's very nice to get away
from the heat in New York."

At 11:06 the *Stockholm* lookout sang out: "Lights to port." Carstens
looked at his radar set. The blip was about 1.8 or 1.9 miles away. Captain

Crowds pack the sidewalks to read the latest news of the Titanic disaster, posted on marquees, including names of some survivors. First reports were so meager and confusing that some papers filled in the blanks with imaginary details of booming sirens, fog and "a crash like an earthquake." In an excess of enthusiasm, The Evening Sun garbled the "facts" and ran the banner headline: ALL SAVED FROM TITANIC AFTER COLLISION. The newspaper went on to report that the Titanic was being taken in tow to Halifax by the liner Virginian.

Nordenson's standing orders were never to allow another vessel to come within a mile of the *Stockholm.* Carstens decided to increase his margin of safety. He swung the *Stockholm* 20° to starboard and steadied her on her new course.

The *Andrea Doria* sighted the *Stockholm* as she was swinging to starboard. "She is turning, she is turning!" the third officer screamed to Captain Calamai. "She is showing the red light! She is coming toward us!"

Captain Calamai could not believe what he was seeing. "All left!" he shouted to the helmsman.

At that moment, still oblivious of danger, Carstens walked to the bridge wing and got a shock to equal Captain Calamai's. He was no longer looking at a blip on a radar but a ship, and suddenly, incredibly, that ship was veering across his bow—a giant black ship sparkling with lights—and among those lights was a green light. Carstens lunged at his engine-room telegraph and signaled full speed astern, shouting "Hard a-starboard."

At 11:09 on this vast ocean the two ships occupied the same space at the same time. The *Stockholm's* clipper bow, constructed of two rows of inch-thick steel plating separated by an air space of two feet, cut through the *Andrea Doria* like an ax blade. A fiery shower of sparks shot up into the night as steel screamed against steel. Half-blinded by the dazzle, Carstens lurched into the wheelhouse and pressed the alarm button to signal the closing of the watertight doors. The *Stockholm's* bow penetrated the starboard side of the *Andrea Doria* for nearly 30 feet—one third the width of the ship—below the bridge, extending down to the double bottom. An inverted triangle, the gash was about 40 feet wide at the top, tapering down to a point. After agonizing seconds, the *Andrea Doria,* her engines running at full speed ahead, tore away from what was left of the *Stockholm's* bow.

Captain Calamai staggered to the wing of the bridge in time to see the *Stockholm* disappear beyond the stern of his ship. Then he rushed to the wheelhouse and jerked the engine telegraph to full stop, shouting to Franchini: "The watertight doors—see that they're closed!"

They were, but in the first minute after the two ships separated, Captain Calamai suddenly realized that the *Andrea Doria* had not righted herself. He checked the trim indicator: 18° to starboard, with the needle creeping, 19°, 20°.

Calamai called the engine room for a report. The starboard turbine motors had been ruptured. But the fatal damage had been done in the compartment immediately forward of the generator room, which contained 10 huge tanks with a capacity of 1,000 tons of fuel oil. Near the end of the voyage the 10 fuel tanks were empty. In piercing the five tanks on the starboard side, the *Stockholm* had allowed 240,000 gallons, or 500 tons, of sea water to rush into them, providing an intolerable dead weight on one side of the ship while the air-filled port tanks lifted the other side out of the sea.

The *Andrea Doria* was divided into 11 watertight chambers with bulkheads extending from the double bottom up to A deck. At anything up to a 15° list the compartments would contain all flooding. But at a 20° list the water would flow from one flooded compartment to another. The

"A deed for which a Hun would blush"

Morte—so read the apocalyptic signature on telegrams reportedly received by a number of passengers just before they boarded the sumptuous British liner *Lusitania* at New York on May 1, 1915. The anonymous and mysterious telegrams warned of impending disaster. Multimillionaire sportsman Alfred G. Vanderbilt was said to have been advised: "Have it on definite authority the *Lusitania* is to be torpedoed. You had better cancel passage immediately."

Cunard officials denied to reporters that any such telegrams had been received. Dockside rumors of these missives of doom nonetheless reinforced the sobering notice that had appeared as an advertisement in the morning

The Lusitania arrives in New York on September 7, 1907, on her maiden voyage. "More beautiful than Solomon's Temple," one admirer said of her. "And big enough to hold all his wives," he added. It was nearly eight years later, when she had made some 200 crossings, that she sailed from the same pier to disaster.

newspapers: the Imperial German Embassy in Washington had reminded Atlantic travelers that a state of war existed between Germany and Great Britain and that vessels flying the flag of Britain or her allies were subject to destruction. Persons entering the war zone encompassing the British Isles therefore did so at their own risk.

But neither Vanderbilt nor most of the other 1,256 passengers were greatly concerned. No German submarine would dare to attack a passenger ship, especially one carrying hundreds of Americans. Anyway, no submarine built could outrun old "Lucy," thrice winner of the coveted Blue Riband as the fastest transatlantic liner. The passengers might have been more anxious had they known that munitions were being shipped in the ship's hold to England.

Threats or no, the *Lusitania* departed for Liverpool at 12:30 p.m. on May Day, 1915. Five days later she crossed into the war zone southwest of Ireland. Routine precautionary steps were taken: the lifeboats were swung out and their

tarpaulin covers removed. The evening of May 6, an urgent wireless message from the British Admiralty—the first of four—warned of U-boat activity in the area.

Aside from posting extra lookouts, Captain William T. Turner paid no heed to the warnings. In fact, he did just what he ought not to have done that fateful morning of May 7. He nonchalantly ignored or misinterpreted the most vital of all wartime Admiralty instructions—maintain maximum speed, keep clear of headlands, steam in mid-channel, steer a zigzag course. Instead, he slowed to a leisurely 18 knots and hugged the coast within half a mile of the Coningbeg Lightship, near an area where submarines had been reported. Rather than elude any attacker by zigzagging, he set a relatively straight course, making his ship an easy target.

Nearby, off the Old Head of Kinsale, Kapitänleutnant Walther Schwieger of the German submarine *U-20* was running on the surface, concluding a week-long patrol. He had already sunk one small schooner and three steamers off the southeast coast of Ireland. At 1:20 p.m. he sighted a ship about 13 miles away. "Starboard ahead four funnels and two masts of a steamer with course at right angles to us," he wrote in his log. "The ship is made out to be large passenger steamer." Submerging, he ran full speed ahead on an intercepting course. An easy kill was assured when the *Lusitania* unsuspectingly altered course toward him.

Without warning, Schwieger fired a bow torpedo. Moments later, at 2:10 p.m., it struck the liner forward on the starboard side, detonated inside the hull, and set off a secondary, even more massive explosion, apparently in the boiler rooms. Listing to starboard, the ship began settling rapidly by the head.

As the vessel tilted forward and down, tons of water poured through the gaping hole and the open lower-deck portholes. Electric power failed, forever trapping screaming passengers in immobile elevators between decks. Life jackets supposedly stored on the boat deck could not be found. Most of the port-side lifeboats could not be launched because of the heavy starboard list. Others on the starboard side were improperly lowered, injuring their occupants or spilling them headlong into the sea. As the bow of the 762-foot ship slowly dipped, it touched the seabed 315 feet below, even as her stern lifted high over the glassy surface.

In 18 minutes she was on the bottom.

Survivors recalled strange, terrible things. A woman was giving birth alone in the chill waters. Hands grasped for deck chairs, lifeboats, oars, planks, anything that would float. Several passengers survived by clinging to an upturned grand piano. Captain Turner clung to a chair until he was rescued hours later. Margaret Gwyer, a recent bride,

A German metalworker produced 100 of these medallions to commemorate the sinking of the Lusitania. One side showed the liner's decks packed with guns and a warplane, and the other depicted a skeleton Cunard agent selling tickets to innocent passengers. British propagandists quickly pressed 250,000 impressions of the medallion to whip up anti-German sentiment.

was sucked into a funnel at the final moment of the *Lusitania*'s plunge, only to be shot forth again—and ultimately reunited with her husband upon landing near his lifeboat.

The survivors of the attack numbered 761. In all, 1,198 died, including 128 Americans and 35 of the 39 infants who had sailed from New York. Alfred G. Vanderbilt, who could not swim a stroke, was last seen standing calmly on deck, holding a purple leather jewel case and dressed as if for the next race at Ascot.

Americans were appalled. "Germany surely must have gone mad," exclaimed the *Richmond Times-Dispatch*. *The Nation* called it "a deed for which a Hun would blush, a Turk be ashamed, and a Barbary pirate apologize." A few officials clamored for war. Anti-German riots erupted as far afield as Canada and South Africa. The Germans themselves exulted in what they saw as a legitimate act of war, the destruction of an armed carrier.

The inquiries that followed turned up all sorts of bizarre suggestions. Had Winston Churchill, the First Lord of the Admiralty, set it all up in Machiavellian hopes of drawing the United States into war? No one could offer the slightest hint of proof. Was the disaster a carefully calculated German ambush? Apparently not; the U-boat skipper seems simply to have stumbled on his prey. Could the negligent Captain Turner have been an agent of the Kaiser? The investigations exonerated him of all culpability; the Germans alone were held responsible for the fate of the *Lusitania*.

And what of the telegrams signed *Morte*? No sender ever stepped forward, and none was discovered. If, in fact, they were received, they must have been the work of a crank who just happened to seize upon precisely the right moment in history to deliver his satanic jest.

Andrea Doria, just like the *Titanic* 44 years earlier, was doomed from the moment she was hit.

At 11:22 both the *Andrea Doria* and the *Stockholm* sent out distress calls. The Coast Guard picked up the SOS at once and relayed the news: "*Andrea Doria* and *Stockholm* collided." In this way the two ships learned of each other's identity.

Even without radio, the *Stockholm* would have learned the name of the *Andrea Doria,* and almost as soon. Bernabe Polanco Garcia, a 36-year-old Spaniard who had signed on as cleaning man in the crew's quarters of the *Stockholm,* had been feeling seasick just a few minutes before the collision. He was halfway up to the open deck for a breath of fresh air when the collison sent him sprawling. He dashed up to the open deck in time to see the *Andrea Doria* veering away, and through the babble of Swedish voices he heard an extraordinary thing—the nearby voice of a child crying in Spanish for her mother: "Donde está Mamá?" Creeping toward the wreckage in the open deck of the bow, Garcia came upon a young girl in torn yellow pajamas.

The girl was Linda Morgan—the daughter of radio news broadcaster Edward P. Morgan—born 14 years before in Mexico and raised in Italy and Spain. Garcia and the Swedish sailors who carried her to the *Stockholm* hospital assumed she was a passenger on their ship, and so did the purser who intercepted them, to whom she spoke in English while giving her name. When he did not find it on the passenger list, he asked where she was from. She replied, "Madrid"—which was no help. At last the shocked girl, looking about her, mumbled: "I was on the *Andrea Doria.* Where am I now?"

Linda Morgan's survival was nothing short of miraculous. The *Stockholm*'s bow crushed to death her eight-year-old sister, Joan, sleeping in the inside bed of cabin 52, but somehow the murderous prow slid under Linda's bed and hurled her from cabin 52 on the *Andrea Doria* to a point some 80 feet behind the peak of the bow of the *Stockholm.* She landed—badly bruised but otherwise sound—behind a curved sea breaker, two and a half feet high, designed to shield electrical equipment from salt spray. In this case it shielded her from flying wreckage. Not far from where Linda was discovered, another *Andrea Doria* passenger was found dead. The unclothed corpse of an elderly woman, Mrs. Walter Carlin of cabin 46, was sitting upright, reddish-brown hair flowing down to her shoulders, left hand outstretched, facing the *Stockholm* like a turned-around figurehead.

At 11:54 Captain Raoul de Beaudéan of the French Line's *Ile de France,* positioned 44 miles from the scene of the accident, radioed the *Andrea Doria:* "Captain *Andrea Doria*—I am going to assist you. Will reach your position 1:35 a.m. Are you sinking? What kind of assistance do you need?"

At the time the message was being sent, a new disaster threatened to make the promised help, two hours away, academic. The hapless *Andrea Doria* had described a rough circle and was drifting sideways, directly for the crushed bow of the *Stockholm.* Captain Nordenson threw the levers of the engine telegraph to full speed astern and shouted to the helmsman for a hard starboard turn. The engines vibrated, the helm was turned, but nothing happened. The chain locker, situated in front of the collision bulkhead, had been smashed open. The two anchor chains had unwound their full 700-foot length and snagged on the sea bed 250 feet below. The *Stockholm* was shackled to the bottom of the ocean.

As helpless now as Captain Calamai, Captain Nordenson watched the *Andrea Doria* bear down on his ship—then veer just enough to pass her, a few hundred yards away.

This crisis past, Nordenson assessed the condition of his vessel. The collision bulkhead was holding, but the forward hold was flooding and the *Stockholm* was nosing down. Nordenson ordered the engine room to empty the ship's forward fresh-water tanks. As 90 tons of water were pumped out, the bow rose, relieving the pressure of the sea on the second watertight bulkhead.

At 12:15 the *Stockholm* received a call from the *Andrea Doria:* "You are one mile from us. Please, if possible, come immediately to pick up our passengers." Nordenson replied: "If you can lower your boats, we can pick you up." Captain Calamai answered: "We are listing too much. Impossible to put boats over side. Please send lifeboats immediately." Nordenson promised lifeboats in 40 minutes.

By 12:30 the list of the *Andrea Doria* had increased to 28°. Somehow, members of the crew swarmed over the davits and managed to launch three boats, with 146-person capacity each. At about 12:45 a lookout on the *Stockholm*'s bridge focused a spotlight on the three lifeboats approaching: they were less than half-filled. Most of the survivors were men. Most of the men were crew. Many wore the white starched jackets of the steward department.

Meanwhile, the United Fruit Company cargo ship *Cape Ann* and the Navy transport *Private William H. Thomas* were close enough to radio a request that the *Andrea Doria* fire rockets.

At about 1:20 the lifeboats from the *Stockholm* began to pull alongside. "Stati calmi, stati calmi," blared the loudspeaker on the *Andrea Doria*. But passengers in orange life jackets leaped into the water, and children were tossed from the rails to be caught as best they could by Swedish sailors with outstretched blankets.

The *Ile de France* arrived at 2:00 with what was needed most: 11 lifeboats, food, blankets, spare cabins, hospital beds. With the *Cape Ann* and the *Thomas* already on the scene, more than 30 lifeboats were filling and refilling with the *Andrea Doria*'s survivors.

By 5 a.m. the *Andrea Doria* had been evacuated except for Captain Calamai and 11 volunteers. The ship was now listing a hopeless 40°. At 5:30 the *Andrea Doria* was abandoned. At 6:05 the *Ile de France* circled the *Andrea Doria* and raised and dipped her colors three times in a farewell salute, then set course for New York. At 9:45 the *Andrea Doria* lurched over on her side. A little after 10, her bow nosed under, and her stern thrust up in the air, uncovering her rudder and twin propellers. Then, at 10:09, she sank.

Of the *Andrea Doria*'s 1,706 passengers and crew, 1,662 were saved. Forty-four were killed by the collision. When the roster was checked, three teen-age crewmen of the *Stockholm* were discovered to have disappeared without a trace from forward cabins on A deck, apparently

In her death throes, the Italian liner Andrea Doria rolls over, exposing a gleaming propeller shaft and propeller 11 hours after colliding with the Stockholm. Just before she slipped beneath the surface, her port-side lifeboats—which had been suspended uselessly in the air when she developed a starboard list—broke away from their davits and floated free. At right the Stockholm, her bows a yawning tangle of steel, arrives in New York for a one-million-dollar repair job.

dragged to the bottom when the bow locker smashed open and those 700-foot anchor chains unwound. They, and two other crewmen who later died of injuries, were the *Stockholm*'s only casualties.

One final scene remained to be played out. After the rescue operation was completed, Captain Nordenson tried to free his ship from her inadvertent mooring. He drove the *Stockholm* back and forth at full power, but her anchors proved stronger than her engines. An acetylene torch was lowered to an officer and his crew in a boat, and they were given orders to cut through the steel links of both anchor chains. Each link weighed 75 pounds. Choppy water made the task not only dangerous but impossible for the men in the bobbing boat. They clambered back on board, where it took more than an hour to burn the chains through at the windlass on the bow.

In the aftermath a number of lengthy inquiries were held. But none could fix a definite blame for the accident. The Swedish government declared itself satisfied that the *Stockholm* was in no way at fault; the Italian government, after interviewing *Andrea Doria* crewmen, did not report their testimony. In an out-of-court settlement of suits between the two companies, the Italian Line agreed to absorb the loss of the $30-million *Andrea Doria*, and the Swedish-American Line absorbed the one-million-dollar cost of a new bow for the *Stockholm*, along with the estimated one-million-dollar loss of business during repairs.

The only culprit everyone could agree on was the fog. Captain Nordenson went on to master another vessel. But Captain Calamai showed how the sea can affect a man when it spins him around in the fog, crushes his ship and turns him into a land animal out of its element. He never sailed again. At the end, he was driven to say the unsayable: "When I was a boy, and all my life, I loved the sea; now I hate it."

Chapter 5

The "Queens" at war

█ t was a good thing that Samuel Cunard was not there to watch. For here was a maiden voyage to make the old steamship entrepreneur wince with pain. The greatest liner ever built, the ultimate Cunarder, was commencing life looking more like a drudge than the monarch whose name she bore. No bands serenaded the *Queen Elizabeth*; no confetti festooned her sides; no gaily waving passengers crowded her decks. Instead of the proud red-and-black Cunard colors, her two enormous funnels were painted a drab Navy gray, as were her superstructure and hull. Silently, secretly, in the cold gloomy dawn of March 2, 1940, the immense vessel crept through the antisubmarine nets at the mouth of Scotland's River Clyde and slipped out to sea.

Britain was at war. German U-boats infested the waters of the North Atlantic, crowding like sea wolves around the British Isles. Somewhere off the Hebrides the German pocket battleship *Deutschland* was known to be prowling. No prize could be greater for a daring Kriegsmarine captain or more crippling to Britain's morale than to sink this greatest of all great liners before she could be put into war duty. But extraordinary precautions had been taken to guard against that possibility.

The *Queen Elizabeth*'s escape to the sea was the climax of many long months of intense preparation and high drama. Indeed, for a time there was a grave question of whether or not she would even go to sea—or would, instead, wind up as a pitiful mountain of scrap, a sacrifice to wartime exigencies.

At the launching on September 27, 1938, Queen Elizabeth, consort of George VI, had christened her namesake and had called her "the noblest vessel ever built in Britain." Her Majesty might fairly have said the world. At 1,031 feet overall, the *Queen Elizabeth* was 12 feet longer than her royal sister ship, the *Queen Mary*, launched four years before. At 83,673 tons, she outranked by 273 tons France's majestic *Normandie*. No other vessels could begin to compare.

Yet when war broke out on September 3, 1939, the *Queen Elizabeth* posed a severe problem for the British government. She lay unfinished in John Brown's fitting-out basin on the Clyde, and the space that she occupied was desperately needed to fit out the Royal Navy's new battleship *Duke of York*, about to be launched at the same yards. Either precious war materials had to be diverted to the *Queen Elizabeth*, so she could be made ready for sea, or she had to be towed away and broken up for steel. In either case, she had to be moved to make room for the *Duke of York*.

Winston Churchill, then First Lord of the Admiralty, personally made the decision to save her. On November 2, the Ministry of Shipping issued the orders to rush her to completion—at least to the stage at which she could be considered seaworthy. She was then to be sent to safety in the United States, where her sister ship, the *Queen Mary*, already lay in dock. There she would await further orders.

As work progressed in strictest secrecy at Clydebank, plans for the *Queen Elizabeth*'s departure were worked out to the finest detail at the Admiralty. Timing was the crucial factor. There would be only two occasions during the following 12 months when tides on the Clyde

Her aft decks carpeted by jubilant soldiers, the Queen Elizabeth arrives in New York in June 1945, carrying 14,000 American and Canadian troops. During the War, the Queen Elizabeth and the Queen Mary transported 1,600,000 men to and from combat zones around the world.

would be high enough to float the monster liner downriver to the open sea. One of the times would be February 26; the other would be six months later, an unacceptable delay in wartime. It would have to be February 26. On that date, within a space of 12 hours, the *Queen Elizabeth* would be nursed out of the fitting-out basin so that the *Duke of York* could be brought in. There would be scant room for error.

In the meantime, a ruse had to be devised as to the *Queen Elizabeth's* destination. Enemy agents were everywhere, and they were assuredly informing Berlin of the race to complete the huge liner. But where was she headed? The British Admiralty decided to dupe the Germans into thinking that she was leaving the Clyde only for her home port of Southampton, where she would complete her fitting-out and then proceed to proving runs off the nearby Solent. It was an idea that was cunningly calculated to attract the Germans. Although Southampton was safe from U-boat attacks, it was well within range of Luftwaffe bombers operating from their bases in Germany.

Early in January 1940, great packing cases of provisions and ship's fittings began arriving in Southampton. Word went out that the King George V dry dock had been reserved for inspection of the *Queen Elizabeth's* hull, propellers and rudder. Hotel rooms were booked in advance for technicians who would participate in the new ship's proving trials off the Solent, and Captain Jack Townley and 400 crewmen, mostly from the *Aquitania*, were signed on for the run south from Scotland. Townley was told that his exact sailing instructions would be delivered by King's messenger only as he weighed anchor, and could be opened only when he was at sea.

On the Clyde, workmen covered the great ship in battleship gray. Degaussing cables—five miles of them—were wired around her hull amidships, and electrical currents were passed through in tests of the system that would neutralize the ship's natural magnetic field, allowing her to sail past enemy lines without detonating their magnetic triggers. Piles of sandbags were arranged on her bridge.

On May 27, 1936, when the *Queen Mary* had first left the Clyde, a gust of wind had shifted her slightly in the narrow channel and she had run aground. To lighten the bigger *Queen Elizabeth* (so she could be floated if the same thing happened to her), all her lifeboats were taken off and towed to deep water at the mouth of the Clyde to wait at a point known as Tail of the Bank.

At noon on February 26, four hours before high tide, tugboats started nudging the great gray lady into midstream. Just off Rashilee Light, the inrushing tide caught her bows and the tugs fought desperately for an hour before they were able to regain control. For 15 miles, they nursed her downriver at barely three miles an hour. And as the early winter night fell, she dropped anchor for the first time off the Tail, took her lifeboats back on board, and began the last of the checks that would consume the hours remaining before the arrival of the King's messenger with her sailing orders.

At 7 a.m. on March 2, the sky was vague with false dawn. Winter lasts long in Scotland, and the sun rises late over the Clyde. In the gloom a Royal Navy launch heaved to and the King's messenger stepped aboard.

The three greatest liners ever built are docked together for the only time, in 1940. Sharing the Cunard pier in New York Harbor with the twin-stacked Queen Elizabeth is the triple-stacked Queen Mary. Beyond her lies the elegant Normandie, pride of the French Line. The new British liner Mauretania at upper left is dwarfed by her three giant rivals.

He turned the sealed orders over to Captain Townley—and in minutes the Queen Elizabeth had eased her way out through the nets at the mouth of the Clyde and was carving a quickening course through the wintry chop toward four destroyers, waiting on her majesty.

The wind was blustery as she began the first of her endless, irregularly timed zigzags, the helmsman spinning the wheel first to the right, then to the left, then to the right. . . . Even at a speed of 24.5 knots—considerably less than her maximum because her engines were not broken in—she was faster than any U-boat. But she was in enemy-infested waters, and if she maintained a straight course or even if she steered a predictable series of zigzags, it was conceivable that a submarine captain could compute an accurate lead and score a deadly torpedo hit. So the Queen Elizabeth zigzagged, her escorts carefully keeping station, modulating their speed to hers until they were 200 miles northwest of Rathlin island at the top of Ireland.

By now the greatest concentration of U-boats had been left behind. With a clacking of signal lights, the destroyers fell away into the dusk and the mighty Queen Elizabeth ruled the darkening ocean alone, all lights out or hooded, a gray mass against a black sea. On board the gray monarch, the 400 crewmen rattled around the vast spaces designed to hold more than 3,500 passengers and crew. Every man had a first-class cabin to himself—if anything could be called first class on that unfinished ship. "We had no carpets, just bare floors, no heating and the light fixtures were just hanging wires," one engineer recalled.

Far behind in Southampton, the crates of labeled ship's fittings and provisions lay unopened on the dock and the reserved hotel rooms remained empty. And on the day that the *Queen Elizabeth* was expected to be in the Solent, the sky filled with Luftwaffe bombers. The British Admiralty's ruse had been successful.

On the morning of March 7, 40 miles east of Fire Island, an American airliner radioed a report of a giant gray ship below zigzagging furiously toward New York Harbor. There were patches of rust where the hastily applied gray paint had already started to peel from her hull and superstructure. By the time she entered the Hudson that afternoon the British Broadcasting Corporation had put out the news that the *Queen Elizabeth* was approaching New York. Thousands upon thousands of people were waiting to greet her. The papers hurried extras into the streets announcing her arrival and calling her the "Empress Incognito."

At a quarter to five, the big gray ship eased into Cunard Pier 90, next to the *Queen Mary*, which had preceded her by 16 months—the sister ships together for the first time. "Many sagas of the sea have begun and ended in our harbour," observed *The New York Times*, "but can the old-timers remember anything to compare with the unheralded arrival of the biggest and fastest liner in the world, after the most daring of all maiden crossings?"

For the *Queen Elizabeth*, for all the liners, it was only the beginning.

Now the great liners were to embark on their greatest adventures of all. Built for the height of luxury and indulgence in peacetime, they were to prove vital to survival in the most awful of all wars. Because they ultimately were able to transport entire divisions of troops at a time, to shift corps and armies from theater to theater in a matter of days, they were instrumental in altering the balance of power at crucial junctures. All this they accomplished at great risk. In waters prowled by U-boats, they were the biggest and most tempting targets afloat—one torpedo could cost the lives of 16,000 soldiers plus some 200 crewmen. Their only defense was secrecy and speed. Statesmen would credit them for shortening the war by as much as a year. But a generation of soldiers would remember the great liner-cum-troopship for other reasons, tasting the sea for the first time aboard the grandest vessels man had ever conceived.

And then, suddenly, hardly two decades after their wartime triumphs, the great liners were destined virtually to disappear from the high seas. By the 1960s the era would be over.

In New York Harbor that chilly early spring of 1940, the two Cunard *Queens* were not alone. Tied up nearby were the Cunarder *Aquitania* and the French Line's *Ile de France* and *Normandie.* With them was the Italian Line's sleek *Rex*, not yet an enemy, but soon to be—and destined for tragedy (page 147). By day, guards patrolled the piers to secure them

The tragic demise of the "Rex"

The death of a great liner was always reason for mourning, and never more so than when she was a sacrifice of war. Such was the fate of the Italian Line's flagship *Rex*, which met her end off the coast of Italy on September 8, 1944. Like the sinking of the *Lusitania* 29 years earlier, the *Rex*'s end served to emphasize how vulnerable a liner could be.

Launched at Genoa in 1932, the *Rex* was the largest, fastest and handsomest ship ever built in Italy. At 51,062 tons she was in a class with the biggest of her British and French competitors. At 29 knots she was fast enough in 1933 to wrest the coveted Blue Riband from the German liner *Bremen* for the fastest westbound transatlantic crossing.

The *Rex* was in home waters when Italy entered the War as a German ally on June 10, 1940. The Italian High Command never seriously considered turning her into a troopship; the narrow Mediterranean was too full of hostile vessels and planes. Instead, the *Rex* was sent to safety, first to Bari and then north to Trieste at the head of the Adriatic. She remained laid up there until the approach of Allied forces in September 1944. Italy had already surrendered, but German armies were still fighting on the peninsula, and German engineers conceived a plan to deny the Allies Trieste as a supply port. They decided to sink the 880-foot *Rex* as a blockship across the mouth of the harbor.

Almost immediately, British reconnaissance planes noted activity on the long-dormant liner, and intelligence specialists guessed at the German tactic. The British were reluctant to sink the vessel and did nothing at first except study ways to balk the Germans. But nothing seemed practical. At last, when she was seen moving slowly inshore along the Gulf of Muggia, it was decided to sacrifice her.

Two waves of Bristol Beaufighters were dispatched to do the job. Flashing down in low-level runs with rockets and 20mm cannon, the first wave scored 59 rocket hits; the second wave added another 64. Blazing fiercely, with a 500-foot column of smoke billowing from her shattered hull, the once-lovely *Rex* rolled over and came to rest in the shallows of Capodistria Bay.

The Rex, pride of the Italian Line, steams slowly through Capodistria Bay south of Trieste on September 8, 1944, as Allied rocket-firing aircraft land their initial rounds wide of the mark.

from sabotage; by night, powerful searchlights played blue-white beams over their hulls and decks. United States intelligence officials had just warned Cunard that German agents might take advantage of America's neutrality to plant bombs aboard the *Queen Mary*. But none of the liners would remain long at the piers. Beleaguered Britain needed troop reinforcements from Canada, Australia and other parts of the Empire to ward off the threatened German invasion and turn the tide of war. And how could these troops be transported save on the Cunarders and the surviving liners of Britain's defeated ally, France?

The *Queen Mary* was the first to enter the War. Shortly after the *Queen Elizabeth* arrived in New York, painters went aboard the *Queen Mary* to cover her with battleship gray as well. Luxury trappings, including six miles of carpeting and 220 cases of china, crystal and silver, were removed to warehouses for the duration. Armament was added to her top decks; soon she would have a total of some 40 guns and other equipment, including 20mm Oerlikon antiaircraft cannon, 12 rocket launchers, range finders and a central gun-control house. Around her waist she donned a degaussing girdle of wire to neutralize magnetic mines. When all was ready, dredges sucked the silt from beneath her hull, and on March 21, without notice or fanfare, she sailed away. Her destination was secret, her mission top priority. Three weeks later, on April 17, 1940, some 16,000 miles out of New York, she steamed into Sydney Harbor and put into the Cockatoo Docks and Engineering Company. Australian workmen swarmed over her, and in barely two weeks they managed to triple her passenger capacity. Berths for 5,500 soldiers were added: hammocks were hung in the public rooms and cabins were filled with triple-tiered wooden bunks.

At last she was revamped and on May 5 the first 5,000 Australian troops marched on board and sailed for England. On her return to Sydney less than a month later, she found thousands of other fresh troops boarding other newly arrived and converted liners — the Cunarders *Aquitania* and *Mauretania* (launched in 1939, namesake of the first *Mauretania*), the Canadian Pacific's *Empress of Japan* and *Empress of Canada*, the Royal Mail Line's *Andes*. In late May they all sailed together into the Indian Ocean, the *Queen Mary* leading. They were headed for Britain.

That November the *Queen Elizabeth*, fitted out in New York for lengthy sea duty but with no troop accommodations, sailed around Africa to Singapore. There she was fitted for service as a troop transport. In April 1941 she joined her queenly sister ship conveying Australian troops to the Middle East.

Weather, not U-boats, proved to be the gravest enemy in the Indian Ocean. The *Queens* were built to keep passengers cozy in the North Atlantic, which was chilly even in summer, not to cool them in the torpid heat of the equator. Neither of the ships was air-conditioned, nor did either have ventilation remotely adequate for the climate. The troops aboard, already on edge as they approached the battlefront, baked in the oven-like heat below, day and night, until tempers started exploding in fury. On board the *Queen Elizabeth*, racing through the Indian Ocean bound for Suez in summer 1941, all this anxiety and discomfort resulted in a virtual mutiny.

A familiar wartime chow line stretches through the Queen Mary's first-class restaurant, now turned into a mess-hall cafeteria with narrow tables capable of seating 2,000 men at a time. In an earlier, more peaceful time the wall mural at rear was illuminated with a crystal ship model that tracked the Queen Mary's passage across the Atlantic.

Cramming themselves into and between the bunks of a converted first-class stateroom on the Queen Mary, a group of Air Force men focuses on something of obviously great importance. The official caption reports with a straight face that they are gathered "around a map to detail their exploits in the European theater" —but their enthusiasm makes it look more like a rousing good game of craps.

The trouble started in the mess quarters. Suddenly—no one knows exactly what it was that set them off—the Australian soldiers were heaving crockery around and slugging it out with their fists. The fighting grew in intensity until the troops formed in groups and battled one another with vats of boiling water. At one point, some enraged Aussies seized a hapless cook and stuffed him into an oven that was still hot. The man was severely burned and half-dead before a squad of Royal Marines managed to rescue him. That mindless near-murder seemed to sober the troops. The fighting died down, and the ringleaders were arrested, transferred to the escorting cruiser *Cornwall* and put ashore in Capetown to await punishment by courts-martial.

On their return trips to Australia, the *Queens* carried German prisoners of war—many of them wounded—who fared even worse in the heat. There were burials every four hours as the ships passed through the Red Sea, the hottest part of the voyage. The British did whatever they could, but the conditions were simply too hellish for some of the injured prisoners to survive.

The nature of the War had changed with America's entry on December 7, 1941. The conflict with Japan in Asia and the Pacific suddenly reversed the flow of troop movement. So many Australians and New Zealanders had been shipped out to the North African front that both New Zealand and Australia felt endangered by the Japanese push down through the South Pacific islands. By January 1942, the *Queen Mary* was on her way to New York and the *Queen Elizabeth* to San Francisco to transport American troops to Australia. In the next several months they moved 20,000 U.S. troops into the Pacific front. After the first such voyage, chewing gum was banned from the *Queen Mary*. Her decks had become practically paved with gum wads; caustic soda and scrapers had to be used to remove it from the teak. Soda bottles also posed a problem. Half a million sodas were loaded for GIs on each voyage. To avoid leaving telltale litter in the wake, and because there were wartime shortages of glass, all empties were collected. On one occasion, however, as a voyage neared its end, 499,999 empties had been collected when a security man discovered a GI stuffing a message into number 500,000 preparatory to throwing it overboard. The bottle was painted red, white and blue, and the note gave the date, the name of the ship and a few details of the voyage. It was immediately confiscated and the GI reprimanded.

When they were not carrying GIs to Australia, the *Queens* were hauling them to Glasgow—this time in 15,000-man-division strength. When Churchill visited Washington in December 1941 for talks, General George C. Marshall, U.S. Chief of Staff, put a hard question to the British leader. As Churchill recalled: "He had agreed to send nearly 30,000 American soldiers to Northern Ireland. We had, of course, placed the two *Queens*, the only two 80,000-ton ships in the world, at his disposal for this purpose. General Marshall asked me how many men we ought to put on board, observing that boats, rafts and other means of flotation could only be provided for about 8,000. If this were disregarded they could carry about 16,000. I gave the following answer. 'I can only tell you what we should do. You must judge for yourselves the risks you will run. If it were a direct part of an actual operation we should put all on board

Steaming at more than 28 knots with thousands of American troops on board, the Queen Mary slams into her own escort vessel, the 4,200-ton cruiser H.M.S. Curacao, while approaching Scotland in October 1942. "It felt like a shudder," one soldier later recalled, "as if the Queen Mary had struck a log." The liner suffered relatively minor damage, but the cruiser was cut in two—as this artist's reconstruction indicates—and more than 300 of her crew died.

they could carry. If it were only a question of moving troops in a reasonable time we should not go beyond the limits of the lifeboats, rafts, etc. It is for you to decide.' "

The problem, of course, was a bit more complicated. Cunard officers had calculated that so many men aboard would increase the *Queen Mary's* draft to 44 feet, six inches, well below her maximum load line. Furthermore, as she left New York Harbor, she would have barely enough water even at high tide to scrape over the Hudson Tunnel, running under the river. If she listed at all—and she usually listed heavily in port as GIs packed the rails to gawk at women passing on ferryboats—she would hit the tunnel.

Marshall opted for the maximum number, and Churchill concluded, "Fortune stood our friend." The 16,000 soldiers were ordered to stand exactly according to instructions, without moving, as the *Queen Mary* eased over the tunnel. It worked. The *Queen Elizabeth* followed with another division, and before the summer of 1942 was over, the two ships had slipped out of New York Harbor with two more divisions. They raced stealthily through the U-boat-infested North Atlantic and slipped into the Firth of Clyde without once so much as seeing a periscope or a German aircraft, although Hitler had offered $250,000 and an Iron Cross to any U-boat commander who sank one of the *Queens.*

The great vessels sailed alone, without convoy, depending on speed

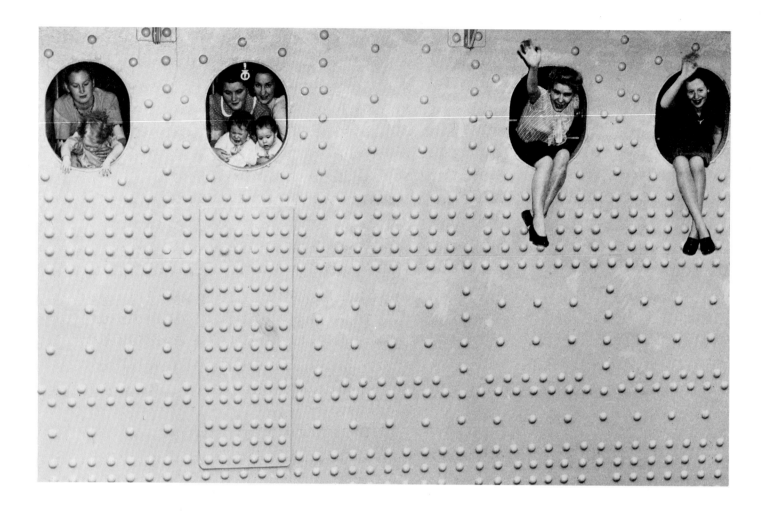

and secrecy—just as had the *Queen Elizabeth* on her initial dash across the Atlantic from the Clyde. The most dangerous stretches were off New York and off Ireland, where U-boats congregated to attack heavy traffic funneling into or streaming out of the ports. No records exist of how many times U-boats sighted one of the Cunard *Queens*. However, there were some close calls.

In March 1942 the *Queen Mary* was delivering 8,398 GIs from New York to Australia only three months after Pearl Harbor. She took a circuitous route through the Caribbean, doing 30 knots and zigzagging out to the open sea by way of the Anegada Passage. Half an hour out of the passage east of the Virgin Islands, the *Queen Mary*'s radio room picked up an SOS from a steamer that had just been attacked by a German U-boat scarcely 10 miles astern. The U-boat commander had missed the *Queen Mary* by only 15 minutes.

On November 9, 1942, the *U-704*, cruising some 200 miles off the west coast of Ireland, reported firing a salvo of four torpedoes at the *Queen Elizabeth* as the liner sped toward the United States with a load of women and children being evacuated from the British Isles. After two minutes and four seconds of silent waiting, the Germans felt the underwater shock of an explosion. Through the raised periscope, the *Elizabeth* was seen to slow to a stop but then resume her course before the subma-

Happily dangling their legs from portholes and holding their babies up for a look, these war brides arriving in New York in February 1946 were among the first wives ferried to the United States on the Queen Mary. On arrival in New York, the women were treated to an escort of planes, while all around swarmed a cavalcade of tooting, water-spraying boats; one tugboat even carried a band that blared out "Here Comes the Bride."

rine could reload bow tubes or position herself to fire stern tubes. The German High Command publicly announced that the *Queen Elizabeth* had been damaged. But the British Admiralty ignored the German claim and there is no evidence to support the story that the *Elizabeth* was hit. The likelihood is that a torpedo exploded prematurely, for word eventually got out that crewmen on board the *Queen Elizabeth* had spotted a monstrous explosion off the port quarter at about the same time that the U-704 had fired the torpedoes.

The *Queen Elizabeth*'s only other brush came in March 1945, off Ireland, when she was transporting GIs. Two destroyer escorts signaled the *Queen Elizabeth* that they had "contacted and were attacking" German U-boats lurking astride her course. "I made up my mind to go ahead," said Captain C. M. Ford, "and three hours later we came upon the scene. We saw depth charges all around us, but that was all."

But there were other perils—to which the *Queen Mary* seemed more susceptible than her younger sister. On the morning of October 2, 1942, as she approached the Clyde, the *Queen Mary* was met by the old cruiser *Curacao*, which had escorted her into port time and again. Seven miles ahead a few destroyers waited to join the escort. But as the great *Queen Mary* and her weathered cruiser escort zigzagged together through the morning hours in full autumn sunlight, one ship or the other misjudged their converging courses and the *Queen Mary* brushed the cruiser's stern, and spun her broadside. The liner's mighty bows sliced through the *Curacao* amidships, spilling bodies into the cold swells. The *Queen Mary* was under orders never to turn back for any reason. On board on this voyage were 10,000 soldiers. Her master had no choice. He steamed on. The destroyers raced in and rescued 102 of the cruiser's men. But 338 had died. A postwar court of inquiry argued endlessly before concluding that two thirds of the blame rested with the doomed *Curacao*, one third with Cunard, which was operating the vessel on behalf of the United States government.

Several months later, in midwinter gales 700 miles off Scotland, bound for Glasgow with a full complement of GIs, the *Queen Mary* was struck by a freak mountainous wave. It slammed her broadside to the seas and for what seemed like minutes she lay on her side in the trough with her upper decks awash. Nobody aboard thought she would ever right herself. Later it was estimated that if she had heeled another five inches the *Queen Mary* would have reached the point of no return, capsized and gone straight to the bottom. But somehow the gray lady righted herself and steamed on. It was never revealed how many of the thousands of GIs on board were injured when they were hurled against the bulkheads and fixtures.

But there were also moments of comedy. Even after the *Queen Mary* had been painted dull gray and her name had been painted over to further disguise her identity, her profile was so distinctive that she could not possibly be mistaken for any other vessel. As she sailed past the Rock of Gibraltar, carrying fresh troops to Suez, the Rock's British defenders challenged her: "What ship? What ship?" The *Queen Mary*'s radio room instantly replied: "What rock? What rock?" Mutual recognition was quickly established.

As the War continued, the troop-carrying capacity of the two *Queens* was exquisitely refined. The innovation that allowed them to transport 16,000 troops was the standee bunk, a tree of metal tubes supporting six canvas stretchers to accommodate six sleeping soldiers. Strong and lightweight, the bunks made it possible to pack twice as many men into the same space occupied by the hammocks and wooden bunks that were installed at the beginning of the War; the standee bunks were also collapsible in order to facilitate cleaning. The Observation Lounge was converted into a maze of five-tiered bunks. Each of her cabins was fitted for 18 triple-tiered units. Only a few rooms were left open for eating. All the other space, including the bottom of the boarded-over swimming pool, was filled to capacity with a forest of standee frames. Three GIs rotated shifts in each bunk over 24-hour periods. Meals were served in 45-minute shifts starting at 6:30 a.m. and as each GI left the dining rooms he carried sandwiches for his lunch. Thirty thousand eggs were boiled every morning. The troops spent the hours between meals playing impromptu card games and shooting dice, and seeing repeated showings of films—one Cunard crewman saw *Pride and Prejudice* 120 times.

On three separate occasions, Churchill crossed the Atlantic aboard the *Queen Mary*. On August 5, 1943, he traveled on the liner to the Quebec Conference to plan the invasion of Normandy. He had brought along models of the "Mulberry Harbors"—artificial harbors that were to be used on the beaches of Normandy to facilitate the landing of men and equipment on coastlines where no protected landing zones existed. Churchill was determined to test their use and did so in his bathtub. While an admiral and a general made waves in the tub, Churchill floated the harbors around and around until 2 a.m.—making it necessary for his wife, Clementine, to go next door to take a bath in the suite of Brigadier and Mrs. Orde Wingate.

During the War the two *Queens* carried some one and one half million soldiers. The *Queen Mary* crossed the Atlantic 86 times, and produced the War's most memorably brief log entry:

"New York to Gourock (Clyde), 16,683 souls aboard. New York 25 July 1943. Gourock 30 July, 1943. 3,353 miles, 4 days 20 hours 42 minutes. 28.73 knots. The greatest number of human beings ever embarked on one vessel."

Churchill concluded: "Built for the arts of peace and to link the Old World with the New, the *Queens* challenged the fury of Hitlerism in the Battle of the Atlantic. Without their aid the day of final victory must unquestionably have been postponed."

At long last, the War was over, and the great liners returned to North Atlantic passenger service. The first civilian passengers were war brides who were heading west to the New World of their GI husbands, and tourists who were heading east to the Old World to see what all the fuss had been about. During the first 18 months after the War the *Queen Mary* carried 12,886 GI brides and their children to the United States, and 10,000 more to Canada. They did not all come over at once, of course. One of the first of the brides to cross the Atlantic was Mrs. Emily Glass, who with 10 others, all classified as "hardship cases," accompanied the

Why liners were scrapped

To the layman, the life span of a great liner was incomprehensibly short: a gala maiden voyage, a relatively few years of service, then the scrap heap as a gleaming replacement liner slid down the ways. The *Vaterland/Leviathan*, for one, was in transatlantic service scarcely 11 years before her retirement in 1934—at a time when to all appearances she was as superb a vessel as the day she was launched.

The quick turnover of liners was a simple matter of advancing technology and declining economics, clear enough to the shipowners if not to the passengers. There was no better example of this inexorable process than the case of Britain's Cunard Line in the late 1920s. Cunard entered the period with three of the greatest liners afloat: the 32,000-ton *Mauretania*, the 45,000-ton *Aquitania* and the 52,000-ton *Berengaria*. Yet within just a few years, Cunard had withdrawn these *grandes dames* from service and replaced them with two new 80,000-ton superships, the *Queen Mary* and *Queen Elizabeth*.

The sad fact was that the trio had swiftly become hopelessly obsolete in the fiercely competitive transatlantic market of the day. The French Line, with its magnificent *Ile de France*, launched in 1927, had carried off the palm for luxury; the North German Lloyd Line, with its new 50,000-tonners *Bremen* and *Europa*, had won the Blue Riband for speed; more important, it had taken the lead in frequency of crossings—once a week. The British vessels were up to four knots slower than the Germans, a difference of half a day on each crossing.

Moreover, for all their majestic appearance, the Cunarders suffered from outdated equipment that required increasing maintenance. The sea is a corrosive enemy of all things man-made. The *Mauretania* and her consorts were plagued by a rash of annoying fires due to decrepit wiring. Malfunctioning boilers required constant attention, and broke down with distressing regularity. Trips to dry dock became more frequent. There was a costly conversion from coal to oil, but even then the three Cunarders consumed fuel at a prodigious rate. Adding to all this, as travel patterns changed, was the further expense and difficulty of converting old steerage compartments into tourist-class cabins with toilet facilities and other amenities.

By contrast, the *Queen Mary* and the *Queen Elizabeth* would cross the Atlantic at 30 knots in four and a half days. Twenty-four hours after arriving in New York they would sail again for Southampton—weekly service by Cunard with time to spare. For all their speed and size, they would require little more fuel than the older vessels. And they would be designed from the keel up with the new tourism in mind. On the *Queen Mary*, for example, 776 cabin-class accommodations replaced first and second class, and there were staterooms for another 784 travelers in tourist and 579 in third class, which offered varying degrees of middle-class comfort.

By the time the *Queen Mary* made her maiden voyage in 1936, the original *Mauretania* had already been broken up for scrap; she had served on the transatlantic service for 18 years and completed 269 double crossings, but her day was done. The *Berengaria* was retired two years later, and the *Aquitania*, after noble duty as a World War II transport, made her final voyage to the ship breakers in 1950.

8,800 men of the 82nd Airborne Division to New York shortly after the War was over. She had married a sergeant in the U.S. Army medical corps stationed in England, and the particular hardship that earned her early passage was Stephen, Shawn and Robert Jr., seven-month-old triplets. At sea the Airborne Division's troopers raised $8,800 for the children, to be used as a college fund. "The American soldiers were so wonderful," recalled Mrs. Glass. "They did just about everything, but none volunteered to wash the 36 diapers a day."

In January 1946 the *Queen Mary* put into Southampton to have some of her war trappings removed and special laundry rooms added; the ship's nursery was reopened and a number of collapsible baby high chairs, designed to fit her dining-saloon armchairs, were brought on board. In the smoking room, playpens replaced the lounge chairs; diapers were dried in the emptied D-deck swimming pool. In deference to maternity, no liquor was served on westbound voyages. On February 5, 1946, the *Queen Mary* sailed with 1,706 brides and their 604 children. Most of them were seasick. The captain, Charles G. Illingworth, discovered it was not the effect of the sea alone: "The poor dears had been starved for chocolates. When they found the canteens loaded with sweets, I'm afraid they overindulged."

While the *Queen Mary* was thus engaged, the *Queen Elizabeth* sailed from New York on February 21, 1946, for dry dock at Southampton and conversion at last into the luxury liner she was born to be, six years earlier. Her captain, C. M. Fuller, bid farewell to New York with the fateful observation: "Steamships will not suffer from postwar transocean air travel because of the discomfort of air travel. There is a problem of getting stuck at an aerodrome for days because of fog. You can make planes, but you can't make weather."

In March, Cunard shipyard workers started giving the *Queen Elizabeth* her first coating of red and black paint on her funnels, white on her topsides and black on her hull. Her troopship accommodations were removed and luxury fittings put back into place. She was ready for her first real maiden voyage as a great liner on October 16, 1946, and she was booked solid. Among the passengers were many of those who had secured their reservations eight years earlier for the *Queen Elizabeth*'s original maiden voyage.

By now, the *Queen Mary* was also in the shipyards. On September 29, 1946, she had delivered her last cargo of brides to Canada and had returned to Southampton, making the fastest crossing in her history: three days, 22 hours and 42 minutes, for an average speed of almost 32 knots. She did not sail again for nearly a year, as workmen hauled out her thousands of standee bunks, latrines and mess-hall fittings and replaced them with her original furnishings, stored throughout the War in warehouses in Sydney and New York. While these were installed, other workers holystoned the hobnail boot marks from her teak decks, planed the GI penknife carvings off her handrails, and chipped away at bulkheads daubed with crude signs attesting to the ocean passage of that ubiquitous American, Kilroy.

The combined cost of refitting the two *Queens*, plus the second *Mauretania* and the *Britannic*, came to more than $30 million. But when the job was finished, the results were greeted with unprecedented enthusiasm by a world long held in the fetters of war. A vast new middle class was growing in America, and they all went to Europe—or so it seemed— newlyweds, secretaries, haberdashers and college kids, graying old doughboys and recent GIs. They went to the Old World to enjoy what they had fought for and what their fathers and grandfathers remembered, to sit in cafés along boulevards, in beer halls and bistros, to stroll in villages and cathedrals or simply to gawk. The children and grandchildren of immigrants, most of them, of ragged men and women who had scraped their last coins together to pay for the gruel and straw of steerage, now made the passage in style.

For about $300 in cabin class and $225 in third, they got a taste of first class served up cut-rate, a mini-first-class menu complete with wine and tablecloths, *consommé madrilène* and curly carrots—served by crisply attired waiters. With free-flowing Burgundy, Bordeaux and brandy in cabin class and beer and bourbon in third, it was almost as good as enjoying champagne and caviar in first class.

In her reincarnation, the *Queen Mary* could carry 1,904 passengers: 701 in first class, 478 in cabin class, 725 in third—there was no steerage. Her sister, the *Queen Elizabeth*, could carry 2,082 passengers in about the same proportion. And it seemed that they were always full. In 1949, the *Queen Mary*'s tourist berths were sold out for nearly a year ahead; so were the *Queen Elizabeth*'s. If a passenger favored a particular first-class cabin, a deposit was required six months in advance. For three great years, 1946 through 1949, the *Queens* alone were delivering profits to Cunard to the tune of $50 million a year.

The transatlantic revival was so momentous that the United States decided to become involved, and in a big way. In the early 1950s, three quarters of all first-class transatlantic passengers were Americans. However, only one major liner, the *America*—33,550 tons, completed in 1940—flew the Stars and Stripes. Now on February 8, 1950, at what seemed to be the absolute apex of the Age of Great Liners, the United States Lines laid down the keel for what was to be the most ambitious ship in all of American history, the *United States*.

The design of the *United States* was strongly influenced by the brilliant wartime performance of the *Queen Elizabeth* and *Queen Mary*. Her designer was William Francis Gibbs, who had redesigned the *Vaterland* into the *Leviathan* following World War I. And Gibbs worked closely with the United States Navy to produce a vessel that could function equally well as a floating palace for 2,000 pleasure seekers or a troop ferry for 14,000 GIs.

Viewed through confetti tossed from Manhattan office windows, the liner United States moves up the Hudson before her maiden voyage in 1952. Though by no means spartan, she was— in the words of her designer, William Francis Gibbs—"a ship, not an ancient inn with oaken beams and plaster walls."

To hold her weight down, Gibbs specified the use of massive quantities of aluminum. Her lifeboats and their oars, her deck rail and davits, the 1.2 million rivets driven into her hull—all were aluminum. Even the 1,200 flower vases were of aluminum. And by substituting aluminum wherever possible for wooden fittings, Gibbs also increased the ship's resistance to fire. When Gibbs discovered that a baker had installed his own wooden shelf in the galley, he had an aluminum facsimile made and substituted. For months Gibbs tried to persuade Theodore Steinway to provide a piano sheathed in aluminum. He was not satisfied until Steinway offered to set flame to a gasoline-doused fireproof mahogany piano to prove it would not burn. The only wooden thing aboard, one wit suggested, was the small piece of wood the very superstitious Gibbs carried in his pocket to knock on.

Costs rose alarmingly when special items had to be produced of aluminum just for the *United States*. Baby high chairs that ordinarily cost $20 in wood were handcrafted in aluminum at $250 each. Coat hangers were weighed on household scales, and when aluminum ones were determined to be the lightest, special chromed shoulder pads had to be devised to make them suitable for the expensive clothing of first-class passengers. Gibbs ordered an officer to take down a wood-framed personal photograph so that its frame could be replaced with one of aluminum. A passenger agent joked that he once turned away a would-be passenger because he had a wooden leg.

By his almost obsessive concern about weight, Gibbs was able to eliminate 2,500 tons from the overall topside structure of the *United States*, giving her unprecedented stability. Because of her role as a Naval auxiliary, secrecy attended her birth. The 990-foot hull was constructed behind a plywood fence at Newport News Shipbuilding and Drydock Company. Gibbs was particularly fanatical about concealing the *United States'* engines. Not for a decade would it be known that her eight massive boilers—only six operating at any given time, with two in reserve—heated steam to 980° F. at a pressure of 1,000 pounds per square inch, nearly 300° and 600 pounds per square inch more than in the *Queen Mary* or *Queen Elizabeth*. And it was another four years before it was revealed just how much horsepower the *United States* generated in her great turbines: 240,000, almost 100,000 more than any other vessel.

What the world did learn at once was that the *United States* was very fast. On July 3, 1952, with 2,000 passengers aboard, Captain Harry Manning pointed the *United States* toward Le Havre and opened up. On her third day out she averaged 36.17 knots, or about 41 land miles per hour. As she approached Bishop's Rock, England, the traditional finish line for the Blue Riband, symbolizing supremacy in speed, President Harry Truman's daughter, Margaret, pulled the ship's horn to signal the event and a deep, booming note of triumph went out across the water. For the first time in 100 years—since the Collins liner *Baltic* achieved it in 1852—an American ship held the Blue Riband. Her time of three days, 10 hours and 40 minutes beat the *Queen Mary's* six-year-old record by 12 hours and two minutes.

But the triumph was an illusion. In 1929, just before the stock-market crash, 1,069,000 passengers had traveled across the Atlantic. In 1958

Displaying Neptune and Amphitrite, god and goddess of the sea, enthroned on the pedestal and two Titans battling for a liner atop a globe supported by Victory, this trophy was donated in 1935 by British Member of Parliament Harold Hales as the symbol of the Blue Riband— awarded for supremacy in speed across the Atlantic. A portrait of Hales is set in the center, bordered at left by the Normandie, which held the trophy in 1935, and at right by the United States, the last winner, in 1952. The Great Western, one of the first transatlantic steamers, is seen below.

more people made the passage than in any other single year before: 1.2 million. The statistics were deceptive. When the *United States* made her maiden crossing, *Punch* ran a cartoon that showed a British Comet jetliner flying across the ship's bow, skywriting the message: "Congratulations, sister." Although the Comet then suffered three disastrous crashes and never fulfilled the challenge implicit in the *Punch* cartoon, it was only a matter of months before other jetliners were flying the Atlantic. Passengers in the new planes were whisked smoothly across the ocean in scarcely seven hours. What is more, the air fares were considerably less expensive.

Suddenly, incredibly, the fortunes of the liner reversed. The curtain was coming down. In 1959, just one year after the *United States* set the all-time record for passenger bookings, reservations declined by 25 per cent. By 1962, Cunard was reporting an annual loss of almost five million dollars and was forced to begin selling some of its real-estate properties to make ends meet.

The *United States* was faring little better. It had cost $78 million to build her, and now the United States Lines could not even afford to pay the interest on that amount, much less amortize it. Except at the peak of the summer season, her voyages rarely even paid for themselves. At times, her crew members outnumbered the passengers by three or even four to one. For a while the United States government pumped a subsidy that averaged $9.7 million per year into the *United States*. Then, in November 1969, scarcely 17 years after the triumph of her maiden passage, the *United States* was moth-balled at Newport News, Virginia, and to all intents and purposes, the United States retired from the transatlantic-passenger shipping lanes.

In the offices of the European shipping lines, worried men studied the rising cost curves and the plummeting passenger curves and reached some painful conclusions. The Compagnie Générale Transatlantique, the fabled French Line, had retired the 32-year-old *Ile de France* as uneconomic at the end of 1958, and had constructed a new vessel, the 66,000-ton *France*, in hopes of recapturing past glory. But it swiftly became apparent that the North Atlantic, with a steady stream of passenger jets overhead, was no longer home to the liners; just to scrape by—and that not for long—French Line ships had to spend much of their time on warm-water winter cruises to the Caribbean and elsewhere.

The Dutch, the Italians and the Scandinavians also offered transatlantic service. But their neat, small ships were equally suited for cruise duty, and that was the way they spent a good deal of their time. By the mid-1960s, only the Cunard Line's two great *Queens* still plied the North Atlantic month in, and month out, winter and summer alike. Frequently they sailed more than half empty. With a professional eye for pathos, British magazines started to liken them to deserted English holiday resorts on rainy summer days.

It was costing an average of $50,000 a day to keep the *Queen Mary* in service, leading the Cunard Line toward bankruptcy. At the end of 1965, the *Queen Elizabeth* was ready for a periodic refit. Cunard decided to refurbish her for 10 more years of service, perhaps in a way that would attract cruise passengers as well. When she emerged several months later, every cabin had its own private bath, and there was air conditioning throughout.

All the desperate hopes were swiftly shattered. On one of her voyages, the *Queen Elizabeth* carried only 70 passengers one way and 130 the other. In the first-class lounge, one might take afternoon tea in the company of stewards only.

The Cunard Line's overall losses rose to nearly $20 million in 1966. The line had laid the keel for a new vessel, the *Queen Elizabeth 2;* though she would ply the Atlantic like the somewhat larger *Queens,* she was conceived more as a cruise ship. On May 8, 1967, the captains of the *Queen Mary* and *Queen Elizabeth,* both at sea, received radio instructions to open sealed envelopes and read the contents to their crews. The letters explained in terse corporate language that each of the two liners was losing $1.8 million a year. Cunard was going to scrap them, the *Queen Mary* in the autumn, the *Queen Elizabeth* the following year.

The era of the great liners was over. The world had turned from sea to air travel as surely as a half century earlier it had turned from sail to steam. The haut monde of the great liners had become the jet set and "grand" had become a period adjective.

In late September, 1967, the *Queen Mary,* 31 years old and one of the two largest ships in the world, put out to sea from New York on her last crossing. There were autumnal chrysanthemums on the captain's table. "The voyage," actress Lynn Redgrave declared, speaking for the 1,450 passengers, "was lovely. You almost expected Ginger Rogers and Fred Astaire to appear and dance any minute."

Across the Atlantic, the *Queen Elizabeth,* 27 years old and the largest ship on earth, sailed westward. In the early morning of September 25, the two greatest liners of all time were due to pass in mid-Atlantic for their last farewell. Only a few passengers stayed awake past midnight to observe the event. Silently they clustered on the forward boat decks and searched the horizon.

And there, as the lights of the onrushing ships winked up above the penumbral sea, the liners approached each other at a combined speed of 60 knots, nearly 70 miles an hour. Brilliant lights blazed on the Cunard red and black of the *Queen Mary's* three great stacks, and on the two enormous funnels of the *Queen Elizabeth.* At 2:20 a.m. the air reverberated as the basso-profundo horns sounded a bellowing salute across the narrowing waters. On their respective bridges, the captains of the *Queens* doffed their braided caps as the two mighty ships raced past each other. Then, like a meteor splitting, the two vessels, ablaze with light, disappeared into the night.

British sailors on the aircraft carrier H.M.S. Hermes salute the Queen Mary as she sails down the English Channel in October 1967 on her final voyage. The 31-year-old liner carried 1,040 travelers on a 39-day cruise to Long Beach, California, where she was made into a civic center.

By the late 1960s the era had ended and almost all the great liners were gone. In New York, in Southampton, in Le Havre, the empty piers lay beckoning, as if any day now one of the grand old ships—the *Leviathan*, the *Ile de France*, the *Normandie*, the two *Queens*, *Mary* and *Elizabeth*—might arrive to the tooting of tugs and a fountain of fireboat spray.

Yet the liners live on in history, and in the memories that shape history. They live in the dusty old photo albums of days spent at sea, in the newspaper rotogravures of gala departures and giddy arrivals, in the yellowed shipping-line brochures extolling the delights of transatlantic travel. And what delights they were.

The voyages began with confetti and streamers and a hubbub of boarding and farewells. From Rolls-Royces and Packards stepped the captains of industry, the stars of stage, screen and opera, the politicians, the titled and untitled aristocrats and the *nouveaux riches*.

When the champagne and tumult at last gave way to the open sea, the great ship settled into a world all her own. While the voyage lasted, that world—the only world—was a kaleidoscope of shuffleboard, deck tennis, gymnasiums, squash courts, Turkish baths, dog shows, wine lists, *pâté* and *pâtisseries*, fancy-dress balls, first-night *soirées* and first-morning hangovers and last-night captains' dinners.

It might never have been the real world, but it was a splendid show while it lasted. And, like all great entertainment, it was over too soon.

Possibly a little late in arriving, an expectant passenger prepares to board the Queen Mary for her 1936 maiden trip from Southampton to New York.

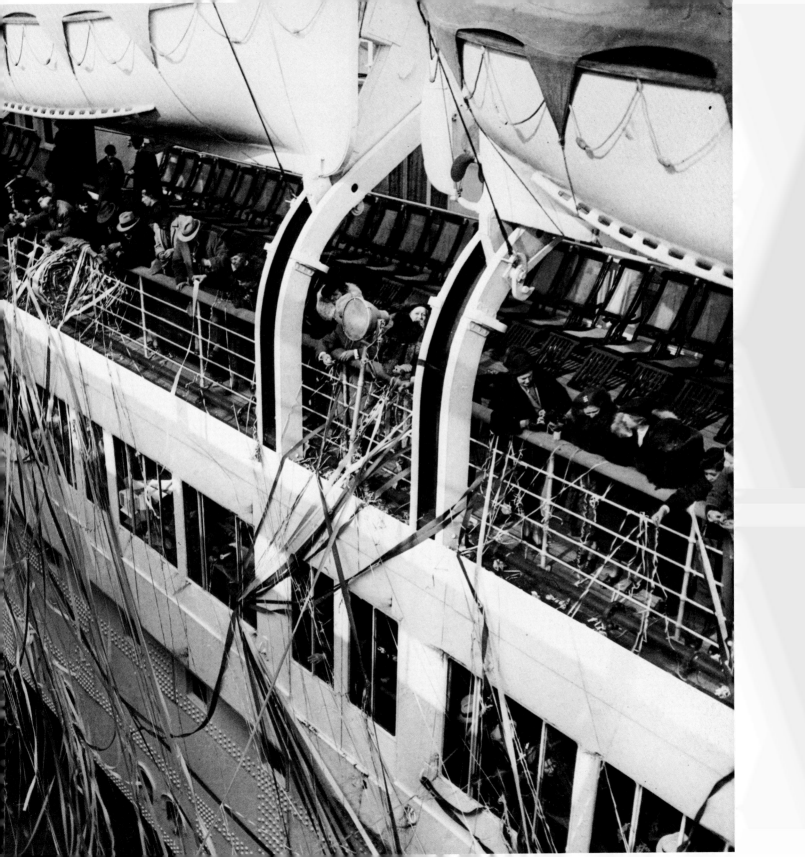

Deck tennis on the Queen Mary offers her passengers a chance to display their athletic prowess—to say nothing of whetting their appetites for another assault on the ship's bars and dining rooms. "Games on shipboard," commented a liner official, "give you just enough healthful exercise and spontaneous laughter to prepare you thoroughly to enjoy the many other diversions of the day."

The fashionable set on the Italian Line's Conte Biancamano whiles away the day with miniature golf, drinks and tea. While a chap with a banjo entertains at right, the gentlemen display a panoply of elegant shipboard haberdashery ranging from a glen-plaid ascot to an awning-stripe blazer nearly matching the parasols.

Bellboys walk the dogs of the Queen Mary's passengers, a frequent ritual. On earlier liners, the ship's butcher took care of the dogs. By the 1920s, a kennelman was hired to oversee canine affairs. Some particularly pampered pets, however, had their own private kennels and were accompanied by their keepers.

went on day and night. They ranged
(clockwise from top) from boxing matches
featuring world heavyweight champion
Primo Carnera to acrobats and the ballet on
the Normandie's stage; from cancan
girls on the Berengaria to horse races on the
Duilio and ballroom dancing aboard
the Conte di Savoia. At center a passenger
posing as a hawker offers unnamed
delights to other revelers in a typical fancy-
dress competition on the Mauretania.

Playing host to six VIPs, Captain Charles
Musgrave Ford presides over the
captain's table on the Queen Elizabeth.
In choosing guests for his table, one
French Line captain confided, "I would
prefer to cope with a good 40-hour
tempest than make a boner in selecting the
charming lady who will sit at my right."

The letdown at journey's end is all the worse for the hellish
scene in the customs shed whether at Southampton, as here, or in
New York. Amid mountains of baggage, crowds of porters
and lines of bewildered passengers, stand the gimlet-eyed customs

men. Although newsreel cameramen were always on hand
(foreground) to capture the celebrities as they disembarked, most
of the passengers felt like Cinderella the morning after
the ball: they were once again the victims of inglorious reality.

Bibliography

Allen, F. L., *Great Pierpont Morgan*. Harper & Bros., 1949.

Angas, William Mack, *Rivalry on the Atlantic*. Lee Furman, 1939.

Appleyard, Rollo, *Charles Parsons: His Life and Work*. Constable, 1933.

Armstrong, Warren, *The Collins Story*. Robert Hale, 1957.

Baarslag, Karl, *SOS: Radio Rescues at Sea*. Methuen, 1937.

Bailey, Thomas A., and Paul B. Ryan, *The Lusitania Disaster*. The Free Press, 1975.

Barbance, Marthe, *Historie de la Compagnie Générale Transatlantique*. Arts et Métiers Graphiques, 1955.

Bathe, Basil W., *Seven Centuries of Sea Travel—From the Crusaders to the Cruises*. Office du Livre, Fribourg, 1973.

Beaudéan, Raoul de, *Captain of the Ile*. McGraw-Hill, 1960.

Beaver, Patrick, *The Big Ship*. Holland America Cruises, no date.

Bemelmans, Ludwig, *The World of Bemelmans*. Viking, 1955.

Blocksidge, Ernest W., *Ships' Boats*. Longmans, Green, 1920.

Blumenschein, Ulrich, *Luxusliner*. Stalling, 1975.

Böer, Friedrich, *Everything about a Ship and Its Cargo*. Verlag Herder, 1969.

Braynard, Frank O.:
Famous American Ships. Hastings House, 1956.
Lives of the Liners. Cornell Maritime Press, 1947.
The Story of the Leviathan. South Street Seaport Museum, Vol. I, 1972; Vol. II, 1974; Vol. III, 1976.

Brinnin, John Malcolm, *The Sway of the Grand Saloon*. Delacorte, 1971.

Cecil, Lamar, *Albert Ballin: Business and Politics in Imperial Germany*. Princeton University Press, 1967.

Churchill, Winston S., *The Second World War*, Vol. III, *The Grand Alliance*. Houghton Mifflin, 1949.

Coleman, Terry, *The Liners*. Putnam's, 1976.

Doenitz, Karl, *Memoirs: Ten Years and Twenty Days* (translated by R. H. Stevens). World, 1959.

Duncan, William J., *R.M.S. Queen Mary: Queen of Queens*. Droke House, 1969.

Emmons, Frederick, *The Atlantic Liners 1925-70*. Bonanza Books, 1972.

Gibbs, C. R. Vernon, *Passenger Liners of the Western Ocean*. Staples Press, 1957.

Greenhill, Basil, *The Great Migration*. Her Majesty's Stationery Office, 1976.

Hancock, H. E., *Wireless at Sea*. Marconi International Marine Communication Company, 1950.

Handlin, Oscar, *The Uprooted*. Grossett & Dunlap, 1951.

History of the U.S.S. Leviathan. Eagle Press, 1919.

Hocking, Charles, *Dictionary of Disasters at Sea during the Age of Steam*. Lloyds Register of Shipping, 1969.

Hodges, Peter, *Royal Navy Warship Camouflage 1939-45*. Almark Publishing, 1973.

Hoehling, A. A. and Mary, *The Last Voyage of the Lusitania*. Popular Library, 1957.

Howe, Irving, *World of Our Fathers*. Simon & Schuster, 1976.

Huldermann, Bernhard, *Albert Ballin*. Cassell, 1922.

Hyde, Francis E., *Cunard and the North Atlantic: 1840-1973*. Humanities Press, 1975.

Jones, Maldwyn Allen, *American Immigration*, University of Chicago Press, 1960.

Kemp, Peter, ed., *The Oxford Companion to Ships and the Sea*. Oxford University Press, 1976.

Kludas, Arnold, *Great Passenger Ships of the World*. Patrick Stephens, Vol. I, 1975; Vol. II, III, 1976; Vol. IV, 1977.

Lacey, Robert, *The Queens of the North Atlantic*. Stein and Day, 1973.

Lord, Walter, *A Night to Remember*. Holt, Rinehart and Winston, 1976.

MacLean, Donald, *The Captain's Bridge*. Doubleday, 1965.

Marcus, Geoffrey, *The Maiden Voyage*. Viking, 1969.

Maxtone-Graham, John, *The Only Way to Cross*. Macmillan, 1972.

Mencken, August, *First-Class Passengers*. Knopf, 1938.

Miller, Byron S., *Sail, Steam and Splendour*. NY Times Books, 1977.

Moscow, Alvin, *Collision Course*. Putnam's, 1959.

Newell, Gordon, *Ocean Liners of the 20th Century*. Bonanza Books, 1963.

Newman, Joseph, directing editor, *200 Years: A Bicentennial History of the U.S.*, Vol. II. U.S. News and World Report Books, 1973.

Ocean Liners of the Past:
Aquitania: No. 3 of Series. Patrick Stephens, 1971.
Normandie: No. 5 of Series. Patrick Stephens, 1972.
Olympic and Titanic: No. 1 of Series. Patrick Stephens, 1970.
Queen Mary: No. 6 of Series. Reprints from "The Shipbuilder and Marine Engine-Builder," Patrick Stephens, 1972.

Padfield, Peter:
An Agony of Collisions. Hodder and Stoughton, 1966.
The Titanic and the Californian. John Day, 1965.

Le Paquebot "Normandie." L'Illustration, June 1935.

Phillips-Birt, Douglas, *When Luxury Went to Sea*. David and Charles, 1971.

Potter, Neil, and Jack Frost:
The Elizabeth. George G. Harrap, 1965.
The Queen Mary. John Day, 1961.

Reynolds, Clark G., *Command of the Sea*. Robert Hale, 1974.

Schaap, Dick, *A Bridge to the Seven Seas*. Holland America Cruises, 1973.

Stanford, Don, *The Ile de France*. Appleton-Century-Crofts, 1960.

Steiner, Edward, *On the Trail of the Immigrant*. Fleming H. Revell, 1906.

Stevenson, Robert Louis, *From Scotland to Silverado* (edited by Janies Hart). Belknap, 1966.

Stevens, Leonard A., *The Elizabeth: Passage of a Queen*. Knopf, 1968.

Thoreux, Pierre, *J'ai Commandé "Normandie."* Presse de la Cité, 1963.

Topham, Anne, *Chronicles of the Prussian Court*. Hutchinson, 1926.

Tute, Warren, *Atlantic Conquest*. Little, Brown, 1962.

Tyler, David Budlong, *Steam Conquers the Atlantic*. D. Appleton-Century, 1939.

Villiers, Alan, *Wild Ocean*. McGraw-Hill, 1957.

Wall, Robert, *Ocean Liners*. E. P. Dutton, 1977.

Walker, J. Bernard, *An Unsinkable Titanic*. Dodd Mead, 1912.

Watt, D. S., and Raymond Birt, *The Queen Elizabeth: The World's Greatest Ship*. Winchester, 1947.

Williams, Archibald, *All about Our Wonderful Ships*. Cassell, 1924.

Wilson, V. S. Fellowes, *The Longest Ships of the World*. Crosby Lockwood, 1928.

Winocour, Jack, ed., *The Story of the Titanic*. Dover, 1960.

Wolfe, Thomas, *Of Time and the River*. Scribner, 1935.

Woon, Basil, *The Frantic Atlantic*. Knopf, 1927.

Picture Credits

The sources for the illustrations in this book are shown below. Credits from left to right are separated by semicolons, from top to bottom by dashes.

Cover: Peabody Museum of Salem.
Front and back end papers: Drawing by Nicholas Fasciano.
3: Charlie Brown courtesy National Museum of History and Technology, Smithsonian Institution. 7: *Normandie*, Adolphe Cassandre © A.D.A.G.P., Paris, 1978, courtesy Compagnie générale maritime. 8: Peabody Museum of Salem. 9: Quarto Publishing Ltd., London, courtesy Cunard Archives, Liverpool. 10, 11: Bildarchiv Preussischer Kulturbesitz courtesy Kuntsbibliothek der Staatlichen Museen, Berlin. 12: David Lees courtesy Museo Civico, Treviso. 13: Quarto Publishing Ltd., London, courtesy Holland America Cruises, Rotterdam. 14, 15: Peabody Museum of Salem. 16, 17: I. N. Phelps Stokes Collection, Prints Division, The New York Public Library, Astor, Lenox and Tilden Foundations. 19: Musée du Québec. 20: Courtesy The Mariners Museum of Newport News, Virginia—Smithsonian Institution neg. no. 45434-A. 22: Cunard Archives, Liverpool University. 25: Derek Bayes courtesy National Maritime Museum, London. 26: Paulus Leeser courtesy Frank O. Braynard Collection. 27: Derek Bayes courtesy National Maritime Museum, London. 28: Frank Lerner courtesy New York Chamber of Commerce and Industry. 29: Courtesy The New-York Historical Society, New York City. 30: Peabody Museum of Salem. 31: Library of Congress. 32, 33: Paulus Leeser courtesy Walter Lord Collection (inset); Harry T. Peters Collection, Museum of the City of New York. 34, 35: Library of Congress. 36: Cunard Archives, Liverpool University. 39: Steamship Historical Society Library, University of Baltimore—from *Charles Parsons, His Life and Work* by Rollo Appleyard, Constable and Co. Ltd., London, 1933. 40, 41: From an album in George Eastman House, Rochester, New York, Smithsonian Institution (2), neg. nos. 47625F and 47629. 42, 43: Peabody Museum of Salem—Derek Bayes courtesy National Maritime Museum, London. 44, 45: *The Illustrated London News*. 46, 47: Collection of Business Americana, Smithsonian Institution; Peabody Museum of Salem. 48, 49: Peabody Museum of Salem; courtesy The New-York Historical Society, New York City. 50, 51: Peabody Museum of Salem. 52: Museum für Hamburgische Geschichte. 53: Arnold Kludas Collection. 54: Henry Groskinsky courtesy Frank O. Braynard Collection. 55, 56, 57: Hapag-Lloyd, Hamburg. 58: Library of Congress. 59: Steamship Historical Society Library, University of Baltimore; Compagnie générale maritime, Paris—Museum of the City of New York. 61: Elisabeth Kraemer courtesy Hapag-Lloyd, Hamburg. 62: Peabody Museum of Salem. 63: Paulus Leeser courtesy Frank O. Braynard Collection. 64, 65: Henry Groskinsky courtesy Frank O. Braynard Collection. 68, 69: National Archives. 71: National Archives—Eileen Tweedy courtesy Imperial War Museum, London. 73: Drawing by Peter McGinn. 74: Underwood & Underwood. 75 through 79: Paulus Leeser courtesy Frank O. Braynard Collection. 81, 82: Copied from *L'Illustration, Le Normandie* Special Issue. 83 through 86: Drawing by John Batchelor. 87, 88, 89: Copied from *L'Illustration, Le Normandie* Special Issue. 90, 91: The Byron Collection, Museum of the City of New York. 92: Compagnie générale maritime, Paris. 94, 95: Photo Bibliothèque nationale, Paris—copied from *Chantiers de l'Atlantique*, Saint-Nazaire. 96: Compagnie géné- rale maritime, Paris. 98: Peabody Museum of Salem. 99: Culver Pictures. 100, 102: Compagnie générale maritime, Paris. 103, 104: The Byron Collection, Museum of the City of New York. 105: Compagnie générale maritime, Paris; The Byron Collection, Museum of the City of New York. 107: Compagnie générale maritime, Paris. 108, 109: Courtesy The Mariners Museum of Newport News, Virginia. 112, 113: Brown Brothers. 114, 115: Alfred Eisenstaedt for LIFE. 116, 117: Peabody Museum of Salem. 120: UPI. 121: Peabody Museum of Salem. 123, 125: Popperfoto, London. 126, 127: *The Illustrated London News*. 128, 129: Paulus Leeser courtesy Walter Lord Collection. 130: Brown Brothers. 131: Picture Collection, The New York Public Library, Astor, Lenox and Tilden Foundations. 132: Radio Times Hulton Picture Library, London. 134, 135, 136: Brown Brothers. 137: Private Collection. 140, 141: H. Trask, Wide World Photos; Howard Sochurek for LIFE. 142: Wide World Photos. 145: Brown Brothers. 147, 149: Imperial War Museum, London. 151: Cunard Archives, Liverpool University. 152: UPI. 156, 157: Brown Brothers. 158: Paulus Leeser courtesy American Merchant Marine Museum. 160, 161: Central Press Photos Ltd., London. 162, 163: Radio Times Hulton Picture Library, London; UPI. 164: UPI—Lorenzo Volante/Agenzia Leoni, Genoa. 165: Radio Times Hulton Picture Library, London. 166: Farabola, Milan; Compagnie générale maritime, Paris—Farabola, Milan; Sport and General Ltd., London, courtesy Cunard Archives, Liverpool University; Roger Schall—Radio Times Hulton Picture Library, London; Compagnie générale maritime, Paris. 167: Alfred Eisenstaedt for LIFE. 168, 169: Courtesy National Railway Museum, York, England.

Acknowledgments

The index for this book was prepared by Sara Hannum Chase. The editors wish to thank the following artists: John Batchelor (pages 80-89) and Nicholas Fasciano (end-paper maps).

The editors also wish to thank: In Germany: Professor Michael Salewski, Bonn; Hans-Jürgen Buchheister and Erika Lisson, Hapag-Lloyd, Bremen; Arnold Kludas, Deutsches Schiffahrtsmuseum, Bremerhaven; Harro Christiansen, Blohm & Voss, Rolf Finck, Hapag-Lloyd, Professor Kurt Illies and Walter Kresse, Museum für Hamburgische Geschichte, Hamburg; Jürgen Meyer, Altonaer Museum, Hamburg-Altona; Ulrich Blumenschein, Oberkirch; Herbert Bischoff, Rheinfeld; Professor Jürgen Rohwer, Bibliothek für Zeitgeschichte, Stuttgart. In Italy: Annamaria Ghiazza, Italia Societá di Navigazione, Genoa; Professor Luigi Menegazzi, Director, Museo Civico "L. Bailo," Treviso; Ennio Vasta, Societá di Navigazione Lloyd-Triestino, Trieste. In London: J. C. Mitchell, Chairman, Cunard Line Ltd.; H. E. Bray, The Illustrated London News; T. C. Charman and George Clout, Printed Books, E. C. Hine and J. W. Pavey, Photographic Department, Imperial War Museum; E. H. H. Archibald, Curator of Oil Paintings, David Lyon, Draught Room, Joan Moore, Photographic Services, G. A. Osbon and Denis Stonham, Department of Prints and Drawings, National Maritime Museum; Roger Daniels, Quarto Publishing Ltd.; Patrick Howarth, Royal National Lifeboat Institution; John A. Bagley, Assistant Keeper, Department of Transport, R. J. Law, Deputy Keeper, Department of Mechanical and Civil Engineering, J. T. Roome and Thomas Wright, Assistant Keeper, Department of Transport, The Science Museum; Paul Rogers, Public Relations Department, Trafalgar House Group; Lesley Coleman; the Lord Mancroft; Peter Pryce. Also in the United Kingdom: Alan Hedgley, Public Affairs Manager, Harland & Wolff Ltd., Belfast; Robert W. Wall, Bristol; the late Captain J. E. Woolfenden, R.N.R., East Sussex; Anthony S. E. Browning, Keeper of Technology, Glasgow Museums and Art Galleries, Glasgow, Scotland; John R. Hume, University of Strathclyde, Glasgow; Michael Moss, Archivist, University of Glasgow; the Earl of Rosse, Birr Castle, Ireland; Michael Cook, Archivist, and Kevin Mahoney, Archives Assistant, Liverpool University; Janet Smith, Record Office, Liverpool; Professor Francis E. Hyde, West Kirby, Merseyside; A. G. Osler, Keeper of Shipping, Science Museum, Newcastle upon Tyne; Robert S. Taylor, Assistant Keeper of Engineering, Tyne and Wear County Council Museums, Newcastle upon Tyne; Kenneth Graham and A. J. Mitchener, Cunard Line Ltd., Southampton; Captain W. E. Warwick, R.N.R. (Ret.), Surrey; A. R. Arrowsmith, Richardsons, Westgarth and Co., Ltd., Wallsend, Tyne and Wear; E. Tuner, Reyrolle Parsons Ltd., Hebburn, Tyne and Wear; C. P. Atkins, Librarian, National Railway Museum, York. In New York: Esther Brumberg, Photography Department, Museum of the City of New York; Wendy Shadwell, Curator of Prints, The New-York Historical Society; Clifford Morgan, Director, Public Relations, United States Lines; Stephen Lash, Walter Lord; John Maxtone-Graham. In Paris: Jean Marie, Former President, Académie de la Marine; René Bouvard, Historiographe, Claude Breitschmitt, Annie Gehl, Service Relations Extérieures, and Pierre de Taulignan, Chef du Service de Presse et des Relations Extérieures, Compagnie Générale Maritime; Gérard Baschet, Editions de L'Illustration; Denise Chaussegroux, Researcher, and Hervé Cras, Director for Documentary Studies, Musée de la Marine; Commandant Georges Croisile; Commissaire André Faure; Guy Dal Piaz. Elsewhere in France: Gérard de Sérigny, Bordeaux; Commandant Jean Henry, Le Cannet; Louis Seignard, Chantiers de l'Atlantique, Saint-Nazaire; Michel Cuisine, Le Havre; Commandant Raymond Agnieray, Wissant.

The editors also wish to thank: Larry Duane Gilmore, Carolyn Ritger, John Sands, Susan Turner, The Mariners Museum of Newport News, Va.; Kathy Flynn, Mark Sexton, Philip C. F. Smith, Peabody Museum, Salem, Mass.; Laura Brown, James Foster, Steamship Society of Baltimore, Md.; Mrs. Charles Hogan, Poughkeepsie, N.Y.; Francis D. Roche, Museum Technician, National Museum of History and Technology, Smithsonian Institution, Washington, D.C.; Kenneth Schultz, Hoboken, N.J.; William H. Tantum IV, Vice President, Titanic Historical Society, Inc., Riverside, Conn.

Quotations from The Sway of the Grand Saloon by John Malcolm Brinnin, reprinted by permission of Delacorte Press/Seymour Lawrence, copyright © 1971 by John Malcolm Brinnin. Other particularly valuable sources of quotations and information were: The Story of the Leviathan by Frank O. Braynard, A Night to Remember by Walter Lord, The Only Way to Cross by John Maxtone-Graham and Collision Course by Alvin Moscow.

Index

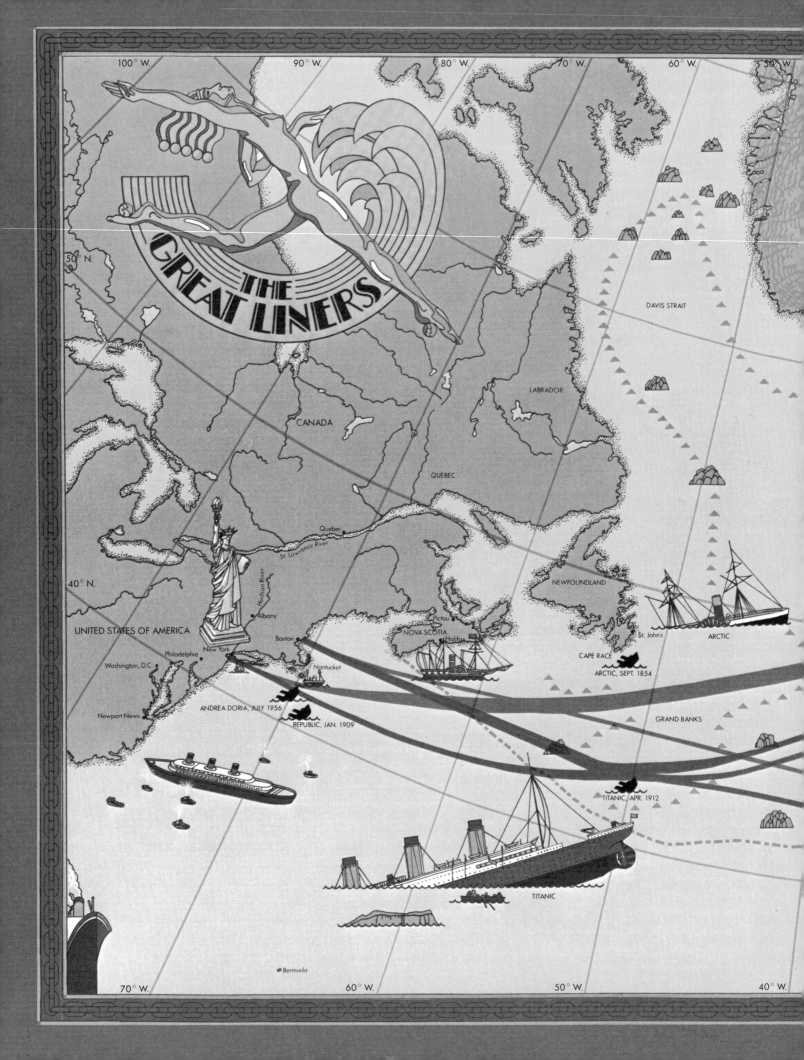